THE FEMALE LEAD

THE FEMALE LEAD

WOMEN WHO SHAPE OUR WORLD

THE FEMALE LEAD

Congratulations - Your school has been nominated to receive The Female Lead – 60 Iconic Women who are shaping the world and sharing their personal stories and diverse achievements in beautiful film and print

The Female Lead is a non-profit organisation dedicated to highlighting the breadth of female achievement across the world today, in order to offer girls inspiring role models and practical guidance around life and career. We have created a teaching pack, featuring the images and stories in our book, together with 60 films and educational resources. All of this is shared free-of-charge to schools across the UK, thanks to many people's generous donations. **Your school has been nominated (by a current or former pupil, parent or member of staff) and we're delighted to share a gifted copy of the book.**

The Female Lead book features icons including Jo Malone, Christiane Amanpour, Meryl Streep and Ava DuVernay, with powerful portraits created by world-renowned photographer, Brigitte Lacombe.

We have collaborated with the Mulberry School for Girls to create a set of teaching resources to bring The Female Lead book and films into the classroom. The purpose of these resources is twofold: to encourage students to engage with the stories of the 60 Female Leads and to enable students to find in these women's stories resources which will help them on their own journeys to success.

The book and rich archive of films are designed to be an active classroom resource and you will find the full teaching pack and downloads available on our website: www.thefemalelead.com/icon-series

The teaching pack lends itself to students' careers learning, and works well within a PSHE programme. The pack has been designed for all pupils, as we believe creating access to a broader range of female role models is of immense value to both boys and girls. We will continue to update our schools pack, so please do keep in touch. We want to hear from you. Please use #ShesMyInspiration on social, or get in touch with Rebecca Small: becky@thefemalelead.com

I founded The Female Lead after being invited to speak to businesses and schools about my own career path, as a data science entrepreneur. When talking to young women I observed that, unlike the boys, they struggled to name a living female role model other than their mother, aunt or grandmother. And so The Female Lead was created, to shine a light on the inspirational and often untold stories of amazing women.

I hope that this helps you to empower girls – to make themselves more visible, more confident and inspire them to aim higher and further in their lives and careers. I genuinely believe that "You Can't Be What you Can't See!"

Edwina Dunn
Founder, The Female Lead

THE FEMALE LEAD

WOMEN WHO SHAPE OUR WORLD

BY EDWINA DUNN

PHOTOGRAPHY BY
BRIGITTE LACOMBE

EBURY
PRESS

1 3 5 7 9 10 8 6 4 2

Ebury Press, an imprint of Ebury Publishing,
20 Vauxhall Bridge Road,
London SW1V 2SA

Ebury Publishing is part of the Penguin Random
House group of companies
whose addresses can be found at
global.penguinrandomhouse.com

Penguin
Random House
UK

Every woman in the book was interviewed on film
by Marian Lacombe. These videos can all be seen at
www.thefemalelead.com

First published by Ebury Press in 2017

www.penguin.co.uk

A CIP catalogue record for this book is available
from the British Library

Hardback ISBN 9781785033520

Trade Paperback ISBN 9781785034336

Printed and bound in China by Toppan Leefung

MIX
Paper from
responsible sources
FSC® C018179

CONTENTS

IN TIMES OF CRISIS, VERY OFTEN I SEE WOMEN TAKING THE LEAD, TAKING THE HELM

CHRISTINE LAGARDE, PAGE 25

INTRODUCTION

A celebration of women's achievement, endeavour and diversity, The Female Lead shows how women shape the world. Founded by data science entrepreneur Edwina Dunn, this non-profit project aims to make women's stories more visible, and to provide positive role models for future generations, nurturing young women's confidence and ambition in all spheres. The Female Lead works across three platforms — the website, thefemalelead.com; an outreach programme that puts on workshops in schools, colleges and youth organisations; and this book of interviews with 60 remarkable women. Each interviewee tells her story in her own words, explaining how she became the person she is today and offering her insights into what she has learned along the way. The book is illustrated with powerful, original portraits by world-renowned photographer Brigitte Lacombe, each accompanied by a short filmed interview made by documentary film maker Marian Lacombe.

We three writers entrusted with interviewing the women whose stories make up this book can count up over a century of years between us of interviewing people from all walks of life. But we found, during the course of writing this book, that there wasn't a single interview that didn't give us something new to think about or amaze us in some way, in which we didn't discover a fresh point of view, or marvel at an impressive story. These accounts speak to all women, and the richness and variety of the different personalities profiled in these pages made our work on this project a pleasure.

Each woman was asked to select an item that had particular personal significance for her,

and to explain her choice and its association with her success. A number of the interviewees picked something that had belonged to a female family member whom they admired; others chose objects with symbolic value, such as a wild bird to represent freedom; others settled on something that summed up their professional life or a personal skill or trait or passion. The variety of the objects reflects the eclecticism of the women — and that diversity is one of the key elements of the project.

Our female leads range widely in terms of age. The youngest interviewed was 14 when she spoke to us, and all decades from teens to 70s are represented. They are also diverse

EDWINA DUNN

Founder, The Female Lead

in terms of nationality – the territories they come from include the UK, the US, Europe, Uganda, Afghanistan, Liberia, Iraq, China and North Korea – and in terms of what they do. In the following pages you will meet politicians, activists, businesswomen, scientists, sportswomen, writers and film-makers, as well as a soldier, a firefighter and a model.

There are, however, common threads. One is a frequent element of struggle and the overcoming of adversity. Some of these women have lived through war and suffered its consequences; for others, the battle has been fought in the workplace; for others again, the struggle has been a personal one for success or recognition. All our interviewees are winners, whether their names command global recognition or they are relatively unknown outside their fields, where they invariably challenge old ideas and lead discussion and innovation. They break the mould and, with their determination and courage, inspire others to do likewise.

Something else that unites these women is their grace. They were all unfailingly courteous and generous with their time, and committed to this project's core theme, which is supporting and encouraging young women. Many benefited from having female mentors along the way and are keen for younger women to benefit similarly. All are sensitive and sympathetic to the issues faced by young women in the 21st century, and all are optimistic about the future, especially regarding the lives and roles of the young women who will come after them.

Geraldine Bedell
Rosanna Greenstreet
Hester Lacey

FOREWORD

One of the most pressing questions for the parent — or teacher or mentor — of a young girl is, 'How do I preserve her natural-born curiosity, drive and courage?' All too often we see the vibrant engagement of the emerging girl quashed by low expectations or rigid roles, battered by self-doubt in adolescence or subsumed by the demands of motherhood. In spite of the enormous social gains throughout the last century, women in many societies continue to be denied education, sexual integrity and independence. Inequality is so embedded in culture that unconscious bias infects the encouragement offered even to girls and women lucky enough to have families and teachers rooting for them. The Female Lead offers an antidote to such prejudice. By presenting the stories of 60 ambitious and successful women, this volume offers a rich register of diverse personal histories, interests, challenges and goals. The focus is not on leading others, but on taking the lead in shaping a life of one's own. The power of this volume lies in its presentation of female drive and direction as normal.

This norm cannot be taken for granted. In my early years as a student of psychology I was introduced to disturbing and disorienting bias against 'the female lead' through one particular study. A list of personality traits and a brief questionnaire were sent to three different groups of psychotherapists. Each group included both men and women. The first group was asked to describe the 'mature, healthy, socially competent man'. The second group was asked to describe the 'mature, healthy, socially competent woman'. The third group was asked to describe the 'mature, healthy, socially competent adult' with no gender specified. The first group indicated that the mature, healthy male would be in control of his feelings, rational (able to distinguish thought from emotion), assertive, capable of leadership and willing to dominate a situation. The second group agreed that the mature, healthy female would be quick to display emotion, would endorse the emotional rather than logical side of the argument, would be susceptible to influence, would in all likelihood be conceited

11

and spend a great deal of time thinking about her appearance, and would be unlikely to take on a leadership role.

The bias demonstrated by these differences was bad enough, but the real blow came from the third category. The mature, healthy adult turned out to be completely indistinguishable from the mature, healthy male. The mature, healthy female, in other words, was a different kind of creature from a mature, healthy adult. In a culture that incorporates a narrow, less than adult concept of grown women, the effect is of silencing, blindness and constraint – silencing because what she says does not have authority; blindness because the full range of what she is able to do and what she might want to do is denied; and constraint because when she take steps towards autonomy, leadership and control, taking that person outside restricted social norms, she is seen as abnormal, unhealthy.

The focus is not on leading others, but on taking the lead in shaping a life of one's own.

Although this study was done several decades ago, current and strong evidence indicates that these biases persist. Very recent research shows that bias does not just act on us via other people's minds; bias threatens us from the inside, too. We often hear that young women today are higher achievers, more goal-directed and more confident than men; but even women of this century reveal vulnerabilities to bias against female achievement. When women are asked to record their gender at the beginning of a quantitative test, and are in a minority when they take the test, or have just watched a commercial in which women were behaving like airheads, or when they have just tried on a swimsuit as opposed to a sweater,

then they perform less well than comparable women perform on the same test in more neutral conditions. Such cues do not generally affect men, because highlighting their gender does not trigger negative associations about mathematical ability.

Recent research shows that girls and women are particularly vulnerable to bias against the female lead at specific crossroads. The first is in adolescence, when social pressures from friends, parents, adverts, films, television and magazines to have designer looks, to be liked and admired, to be a nice girl, put self-confidence at risk. Although today more and more adolescent girls are encouraged to succeed by teachers and parents, many find that entry to the workforce – the second turning point – is less welcoming. The support their ambition may have enjoyed during formal education disappears in the messier, more public workplace. A third juncture comes with experiences of motherhood, its surrounding social institutions and its profound emotional pull.

Many women, at one stage or another, feel stuck or stranded, confounded about a way forward. Each path has to be mapped according to the dense particularity of a woman's own desires, interests and opportunities. At one time, the buzz word for encouragement was 'role model', but the special challenges to women of competing needs, personal responsiveness and complex attachments, make role models problematic. No one person can draw a life map for another. What Edwina Dunn provides here is a rich register of possible ways forward. None is a universal template, but each account enlarges the sense of what is possible as, in her individual way, a girl comes to lead her own life.

Dr Terri Apter

WHEN YOU'RE A LEADER, PEOPLE LISTEN TO YOU. YOU SEE THINGS AND CALL THEM OUT AND PEOPLE ARE GLAD YOU DID, BECAUSE THEY WERE THINKING THE SAME THING.

NELL MERLINO, PAGE 65

MERYL STREEP

Academy Award-winning actor

MERYL STREEP

Meryl Streep has been nominated for 19 Academy Awards, more than any other actor or actress in history. She has won three times – best supporting actress for *Kramer vs Kramer* (1979) and best actress for *Sophie's Choice* (1982) and again for *The Iron Lady* (2011). Born in New Jersey and educated at Vassar College, Dartmouth College and Yale, Meryl Streep is widely regarded as the leading actress of her generation, not least for her ability to transform herself into a wide range of diverse characters. She has received 29 Golden Globe nominations, more competitive (non-honorary) nominations than any other actor or actress in the history of the award, and won eight times. In 2010, President Barack Obama awarded her the National Medal of Arts and, in 2014, the Presidential Medal of Freedom. She was a founding member of Mothers and Others, an environmental advocacy group, which successfully lobbied Congress for new regulations protecting children from the hazards of pesticide exposure. She has underwritten scholarships at colleges and universities, and funds a screenwriting programme for women over the age of 40 through New York Women in Film. In 2015, she sent every member of Congress a letter and a book, *Equal Means Equal*, supporting the Equal Rights Amendment, a proposed amendment to the US Constitution designed to mandate equal rights for women under the law.

I grew up in New Jersey, in a suburb of a very small town – if there is such a thing – and it was my imagination that took me out of my circumstances and enabled me to understand the lives of other people in a way I found thrilling, whether that was through reading, or the things I saw on TV. I didn't always want to be an actor. I thought I wanted to be a translator at the UN and help people understand each other. In a way, that's what I'm trying to do as an actress – to get deep into someone else's life, to understand what made them feel the way they did and compelled them to move in one direction or the other. I just find it endlessly interesting how different we are and how similar we all are.

Some young people come into acting because they see it as glossy and heightened and more sort-of divine than their existence, and there are plenty of avenues to achieve that. But what interests me, and what interests the actors I admire most, is to understand something about yourself and other people. That other stuff, I've never liked it. I realise now I'm not going to. My mother used to say to me, 'People would give their right arm to walk down that red carpet. Enjoy it!' You just can't change who you are.

In the minds of the aggrieved male population, the word feminism sometimes qualifies as something for them to be defensive about, and I feel that men should be on the side of advancing half the human race.

I got very involved in promoting the film *Suffragette* because it's about a part of our history that's not familiar to everyone, and Sarah Gavron's film told the story authentically, with honesty and beauty. There was some controversy at the time because I was asked in an interview whether I was a feminist and I answered by saying, 'I'm a humanist,' which, to me, encompasses advancing the rights of women and girls – being a feminist – and also being part of the human family. In the minds of the aggrieved male population, the word feminism sometimes qualifies as something for them to be defensive about, and I feel that men should be on the side of advancing half the human race. Until men think of discrimination as a problem that is their own – that's to say, a human problem – I don't think we'll move forward. So that's the challenge. Unless men are also discussing this, I don't think anything changes. It's not just a women's issue – it's an issue for everyone.

On alternate days I feel completely despairing and then I think, 'Wow, look how much has been achieved, how things are moving.' The influencers in our industry are overwhelmingly men – the critics, the directors' branch of the Academy. If the directors' branch of the Academy were overwhelmingly female, there would be a hue and cry about it. Women have 17 per cent of the influence, more or less, in every part of the decision-making process in the movie industry and, inevitably, that's going to decide what kinds of film are made. But the material that comes to me, often in the form of books and plays to be adapted, is still interesting. I'm 66, so I get mostly things for people of that age. There's not a lot, but there are wonderful projects that would never have existed even ten years ago. Twenty years ago, I would have been playing witches and crones and scary old ladies in horror movies.

If I could go back, I'd say, 'Think about the bigger picture.'

Acting and the sort of uncertain freelance career that I've had, going from job to job, never knowing exactly where the next one would be, has allowed me to spend a lot of time with my kids – more than if I'd worked at a desk job and had two weeks off in August and one at Christmas. That's a really tough gig and I don't know how I could have had four kids and done that. Decisions I made in my career were not always based on aesthetic criteria – was it near, was it going to be shot in the summer vacation? Then I would do it. You make all sorts of compromises as an artist in order to have this other thing that you value. My girls and my son and my husband are all way too much in each other's business, I would say, but we're close and that's important. I always tried to stay challenged and work hard but also keep my hand in and stir the pot at home.

I spent far too much time when I was younger thinking about how much I weighed. When I think of the man hours – woman hours – I spent on that subject, it was the biggest waste of the minutes of my life. So if I could go back, I'd say, 'Think about the bigger picture.' Of course, it's a visual medium. We think about our looks. I don't bring a suitcase with my dossier in it to an audition or interview, I bring my body – so you can't moan about the fact that you're judged on your looks – it's a visual medium, it's showbusiness. But the other thing is that you're representing lives, and lives look all different ways, all different shapes. That's one thing I do see is changing and it's really good. It just makes the cultural landscape richer.

Meryl's Object
My wedding ring. At various times it's been so tight that they couldn't get it off for movies, not without surgically removing the finger, so they had to invent other rings to go over it. I love it even more than for the regular reasons. I was in a play at the Public Theater a short while after I was married and, as an actress, you give in your valuables, so I put my wedding ring in my wallet and gave it to the stage manager to put in the safe. At the end of the play they brought it back and I went out into the lobby to say hello to some people and when I came back it was gone. It had been my great grandmother's ring, dating back to 1880-something. Beautiful. My husband took his wedding ring and cut it in half and that's what I have now. It's little, because it's half of his. But it's even better.

LEYMAH GBOWEE

*Activist and winner of the
2011 Nobel Peace Prize*

LEYMAH GBOWEE

Leymah Gbowee is a Liberian peace activist and winner of the Nobel Peace Prize. In 2002, angered by the civil war that had been raging in her country for most of her adult life, the then 30-year-old social worker and mother of four (she now has seven children) organised a march of Christian and Muslim women on the capital, with a sit-in that lasted for months. Thousands of women prayed, camped and went on a sex strike. Their actions led President Charles Taylor, who was responsible for much of the violence, to agree to attend peace negotiations in neighbouring Ghana. When it was evident the talks were getting nowhere, Gbowee organised her 'troops' to blockade the meeting room and hold the negotiators 'hostage' until agreement was reached. The women's actions led to the removal of Taylor and the inauguration of the first woman president of an African country, Ellen Johnson Sirleaf, with whom Gbowee shared the Nobel Peace Prize in 2011.

I was 17 when the Liberian civil war started. I had just finished high school and was planning to be a doctor but the war upended everything. It shortened my horizons. I had been brought up to believe in fairness and opportunity and a world in which everyone had a chance. I grew up in a religious household and I had been taught that God would always be there. Yet suddenly a bullet could undo everything. I couldn't see the point of spending four or five years in medical school. I felt so angry at what was happening that it was impossible to focus on life beyond the immediate present. We just existed. Surviving in a war takes a lot of energy. **I did a basic** three-month social work course because that seemed the most immediate way to help to make things more bearable. In time, I worked with former child soldiers, young people who had been destroyed both physically and emotionally by fighting. Many of them were still carrying shrapnel in their bodies. They had been used and thrown aside. This was happening over and over again. I remember being in a village in south-eastern Liberia when the government sent in a truck to abduct the children so as to teach them how to use an AK47 and make them fight. I was with the mothers, watching their children being taken before their eyes. **By 1998, the second** serious outbreak of fighting had been going on for five years. I felt powerless. I had met women activists from Sierra Leone who claimed that women could change things, but I was very cynical about

their optimism. It was only when I began to work with the wives of ex-combatants that I began to see what they meant. The ex-soldiers were often very violent and angry, but their wives stood up to them. I appreciated then the power women have through our empathy and understanding. We are at the heart of things, observing everyone, seeing their comings and goings, knowing the pains and happiness of the family, the whole community. Yet when tensions arise, the men dismiss all that knowedge and wisdom. They say mothers and daughters can't come, can't be involved. **I realised that not** only can women talk about peace but we can also step out in front and say, 'This is what people need.' I joined a Christian women's group. I had a dream of putting women together across the communities, and we started visiting mosques and talking to Muslim women. Did we lose people because of that? Yes, a lot of Christian women left. But we persisted. There was a lot of work to do to create a movement that would really have some impact. It took us two and a half years to prepare our protest. The important thing, the key to success, was that we had no political agenda. We weren't campaigning to become something. Our objective was very clear – we had a shared vision for peace. That was something we could all support. We were there because we cared about the lives of our children, the livelihood of our families. **In 2002 we marched** on Monrovia, the capital, and we stayed there, praying for peace. Even though there were thousands of us and our protest was very visible, the men still weren't taking much notice. When we started the sex strike, it was out of desperation. We wanted to get across the idea that women were doing something and there was a need to support us. We had no idea the media would be interested. But it became a huge story and that became an opportunity for us to talk about peace.

I had met women activists from Sierra Leone who claimed that women could change things, but I was very cynical about their optimism. It was only when I began to work with the wives of ex-combatants that I began to see what they meant.

The pressure built and talks took place aimed at ending the fighting but it was clear that nothing was coming out of them. There was no real commitment. So we went to the hotel where the talks were being held and sat down outside the room. When they threatened to remove us, we said we would disrobe, which horrified them. To see a married or elderly woman deliberately bare herself is thought to bring down a terrible curse.

We were able to use things that were ours – our empathy, the ways we are perceived, our relationships – to make the men listen. I think it is important that we understand those strengths we have, because, over the last few years, wars have become more than ever about terrorising women. Rape and abuse of women and children are seen as ways to demoralise and disgrace the enemy, to show them that they are unable to take care of their families and homes. It has become an exotic thing to capture women.

It is no longer an option for women to say, 'I'm not a politician.' We need to up our game, to know the issues and do our best to get into the conversation. I see a lot of discomfort from men when there is discussion about women's rights, and a view that women are craving to take over from them, to destroy them. Of course, this is not true, but we are interested in justice. We don't want to be passive, victims, used. When it comes to rehabilitation and reconstruction, girls need to be at the top of the list. The age-old excuse has been that we can't find the good women. It is time for the good women to step up.

Leymah's Object
A cross. The cross is a very powerful symbol of the strength that lies in weakness. Christianity has always been important to me but I had a very deep anger with God for a long while because I felt the protection I had been promised was not there. But then it was religious groups who initially came together to call for peace. For me, the cross has many associations that make sense of what I am doing – it signifies a place of pain, but also of redemption. It reminds me that there is terrible suffering in the world but it is possible to get past that. It makes me think of reconciliation and healing.

Every day I wake up and I am amazed by what has happened to me and the honours that I have had, and I feel guilty, because it seems nothing to do with me and my intellectual ability. Keeping the cross in mind helps me to make sense of that. Those honours are not really for me; they are for peace. I cannot feel arrogant while I keep the cross in mind and I do not have to feel embarrassed. Do I deserve what has happened to me? No. But I will strive to be deserving.

CHRISTINE LAGARDE

Managing director, the International Monetary Fund

CHRISTINE LAGARDE

Christine Lagarde was born in Paris, studied law and has held ministerial positions in the French government, including that of finance and economy minister. She was the first woman to become finance minister of a G7 country. Now she is managing director of the International Monetary Fund, the first woman to be elected to the position, which she took up in 2011. She has been reappointed by the IMF Board for a second term starting 4 July 2016. The IMF, which has its headquarters in Washington DC, has 189 member countries and exists to foster global monetary cooperation, secure financial stability, facilitate international trade, promote high employment and sustainable economic growth, and reduce poverty.

Unfortunately, I am often the only woman in the room. There are a few more women than there were 10 or 15 years ago but finance is still a very male-dominated environment. We are dealing with banks, financial experts, economists, finance ministers and governors of central banks, and in most instances these people are men. I do not think that I am treated differently but I probably had a harder time establishing credibility and being respected, whereas for men these are taken for granted instantly. The probation period for women is probably a little longer and the probation tests are probably a little harder.

In some countries women are not as educated as men. Sisters are prevented from going to school when their brothers are allowed to go to school.

We all like to be liked and being criticised is hard, but you just accept it. You fix it when it is legitimate, you ignore it when it is completely gratuitous, or full of hatred – you move on. Occasionally, I compare with other women and very often we have faced and experienced the same issues. We had to prove ourselves and overcome the almost inherent lack of confidence that I do not think men experience as much as we do.

Studies, including some of our own, show that about half of the women capable of joining the workforce are not joining it because of all sorts of impediments, whether these are cultural hurdles, personal hurdles or issues of childcare.

There are not many days when I get up thinking life is not beautiful. That might be rooted in my education, my faith, and my natural optimism.

There are other reasons as well. In some countries, women are not as educated as men. Sisters are prevented from going to school when their brothers are allowed to go. If you look at some of the low-income countries in particular, that is the case. If you look at some countries of the Middle East, it is a different story. Females are very well educated, but for cultural reasons they are not given the same access as their male counterparts to the job market. So it varies depending on countries. What we see on a cross-country basis for women is certainly hurdles, discrimination, obstacles towards getting an education, setting up businesses, accessing finance, and joining the economy more generally.

We have in quite a few instances convinced countries and their authorities that it is in their interest, and in the interest of the economy and society, to encourage women to have children and work. We have shown that it is better to remove discrimination, to allow the same inheritance and property laws, and to give the same access to finance to both men and women. Quite a few countries are now keen to experiment and to make sure that they derive full benefit from women's talent. I want women to have a choice, and to choose on a completely even-handed basis, on a level playing field. They have the same capacity, the same potential as men, and that should not be hampered.

If there is a collective will to include women – and that is often the case – then there has to be a good analysis of what the situation is, what the numbers are, what the education level is, what the opportunities can be, and what the obstacles may be along the way. Once that map has been drawn, then every effort should be made to remove the obstacles, improve opportunities, support education and set targets. Now, whether you call these targets quotas or participation rates in the labour market does not really matter. But to have objectives, and ways to measure against those objectives, I think is necessary. I used to be against quotas when I was much younger, thinking, 'Why should we not just succeed and participate on our own merits?' Unfortunately, there is such a long way to go that targets, quotas and accountability are needed in order to bridge that gap.

I was very lucky to have a powerful, independent mother – and a smart father as well! My mother was determined to encourage what she called my natural sense of independence – and authority, on occasion. I was the eldest of four siblings and she did not stop me from being the boss in those days. She delegated quite a bit of authority to me at the time and I was babysitting the younger boys when I was four or five years of age. That empowerment from a very early stage has certainly been very helpful to me.

Failure is OK. This is not necessarily accepted in all societies or in all civilisations. But success does not come easily and should not be taken for granted. It is very much about hard work, resilience, determination – it is also about teamwork. Helping others, being helped, operating with others on your team is critically important. Some people will not be helpful and some people will want to promote themselves instead of the group. But that is not a reason to assume that you can succeed on your own. I would also say reach out to other women, including more senior women who have succeeded, and ask them for advice, for support.

How do I achieve balance? There have been times in my life when it was certainly not perfect. I have succeeded at certain levels and I have no regrets about what I have done, but you cannot have it all at the same time. Over the course of your life, you can succeed in many areas and you can try not to hurt, not to damage along the way – I think that is the most important. There are not many days when I get up thinking life is not beautiful. That might be rooted in my education, my faith and my natural optimism. Life has its baggage of hard moments, sorrow, pain, frustrations, but I still think that it is beautiful.

I have observed in many instances that when a society, a corporate organisation or a community is in crisis, very often women are called upon to help, support, fix and rebuild. In times of crisis, very often I see women taking the lead, taking the helm. A good friend of mine who used to be governor of a central bank in Africa used to say, 'Men go to war and women come afterwards to fix it.' Very often, in times of crisis, we call the women!

Christine's Object

A terracotta sculpture of people in a circle. You can put a candle in the centre. It was a gift from my mother, who brought it back from one of her trips to Latin America, and it sits on my desk in Paris. It is a symbol of the team, of collective force, as the people are holding hands in a circle around the source of energy and light, without which we are nothing.

YEONMI PARK

*North Korean
human rights activist*

YEONMI PARK

Yeonmi Park is a human rights activist. She was born in the North Korean city of Hyesan, close to the Chinese border. After her father was imprisoned for trading on the black market, the family were branded criminals and forced to the margins of society. In 2007 Yeonmi and her mother defected from North Korea, eventually finding asylum in South Korea. Since then she has travelled the world to speak out against the brutal communist regime in North Korea, currently led by Kim Jong-un, who inherited the leadership from his father and grandfather. Her memoir, *In Order to Live: A North Korean Girl's Journey to Freedom*, was published in 2015.

When I was growing up, I had no clue that North Korea was a strange place to live. I was told it was perfect. We were hungry, and there was no 24-hour electricity, no internet, no human rights or freedom. At school I learned propaganda, how our enemies – the American bastards and Japanese imperialists – were trying to attack us at any moment. We learned about the power of the regime and of our great leaders.

I thought our Dear Leader was a god. I didn't think he was a human being. I believed he could make miracles and that he could read my mind, so I mustn't think bad thoughts about him. When you live in North Korea, you survive by being paranoid. You are watched and reported on, and people get arrested and disappear for many reasons. We heard of people being executed or sent to prison for watching movies. That's why, when I was very young, my mother told me not even to whisper because the birds and mice could hear you. It was very odd for me, when I came to the West, to see parents answering their children's questions and trying to encourage them to express their thoughts. My upbringing was totally opposite to that.

My mother had been to college in North Korea but she was a housewife. My father had been a party member before he was arrested for being a vendor on the black market. When he was sent to prison, I was around eight or nine, and I was very sad. It felt like the end of the world and I didn't see him for three or four years. I didn't know what injustice was, so I didn't feel any anger at the regime or think it unjust

that he was being tortured and starved. After he was arrested, I couldn't go to school any more. I stayed at home and went to the river to wash our clothes and into nature to find things to eat. We ate grasshoppers and plants and flowers and that's how we survived.

When I was 13 years old, I decided to leave North Korea and asked my mother to come with me. My father was really sick and had leave from the prison to come home – he had to go back once he was healthy again. We didn't have anything to eat but frozen potatoes and we didn't have enough of those. I felt I just couldn't die from disease or starvation. We lived in the border area and could see that China had lights, which we did not. I thought if we went to China we might find something to eat.

The man who bought me offered me a deal, that if I became his mistress, he would buy my mother and bring my father from North Korea.

So, in 2007, my mother and I crossed the river into China. We thought we were going to be shot by the guards at the border but we survived. When we got there, a Chinese trafficker was waiting for us. Some people try to take advantage of North Koreans in China. They rape, sell or even kill us and we dare not complain because we don't want to risk being sent back to North Korea to face imprisonment or execution. The trafficker wanted to have sex with me and I didn't even know what sex was. My mother offered herself instead and she was raped in front of my eyes. She sacrificed herself, the most beautiful thing that any mother can do. After, she was sold for 55 dollars and I was sold for 250 dollars. My mother and I got separated from that moment for four or five months. The man who bought me offered me a deal, that if I became his mistress, he would buy my mother and bring my father from North Korea. I sacrificed myself so that I could be reunited with my parents.

To me everything was new and I felt like a time traveller.

We spent almost two years in China. My father passed away from the colon cancer that he got in prison and then, when I was 15 years old, the man who had bought me let me go. My mother and I knew that if we got out of China, we could find asylum, so we decided to cross the frozen Gobi desert into Mongolia. We chose a winter's night in February, as we thought that no one would suspect that we would be crazy enough to cross when it was really cold. We avoided the guards and followed a compass and then, when that broke, we followed the North Star to freedom.

My whole life was full of horror, full of misery and full of injustice and I could never have imagined this kind of paradise where people don't have to worry about where their next meal is coming from.

In Mongolia we were asked to take off our clothes and they searched us. And then, after several months, we were flown to South Korea and, at the age of 15, I became free for the first time. I had never seen an airport before – I had never even seen an escalator or toilet paper. To me everything was new and I felt like a time traveller. In South Korea they sent me to a resettlement centre for three months and there I learned about all these new things: the internet, how to take a selfie and what was American.

My mother is still living in South Korea but now I am in New York and studying at Columbia University. After I wrote my memoir, I travelled to promote my book and I visited New York many times and decided I would like to live here. I am excited to be living in this city. My whole life was full of horror, full of misery and full of injustice and I could never have imagined this kind of paradise where people don't have to worry about where their next meal is coming from. In North Korea the regime told me what to do and the man who bought me in China told me what to do and, at first, it was very hard to be in charge of my life, but owning yourself is the biggest beauty of life in this free world.

My challenge is to master English and to keep sharing my story, in the hope that it can help to bring change and, somehow, a day when North Korea is free. Then I want to go home.

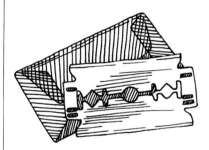

Yeonmi's Object
A razor. When we were crossing the desert, my mother and I carried poison and razors. I kept my razor, which was small and very sharp, in my bag and I would have cut my wrists rather than be arrested and sent back to North Korea where I would die anyway. Killing myself was the only thing to do. No one wants to die, but some people in this world don't have options.

AVA DUVERNAY

*Film director, screenwriter and
founder, ARRAY Film Distribution*

AVA DUVERNAY

Ava DuVernay is a film writer, producer, director and distributor. Her 2014 film *Selma*, about Martin Luther King's 1965 campaign to secure equal voting rights by marching from Selma to Montgomery, Alabama, was nominated for the 2015 Academy Award (Oscar) for Best Picture. Her previous film, *Middle of Nowhere*, won the 2012 Sundance Film Festival Best Director Award. She graduated from the University of California, Los Angeles with a double major in English and African American studies, and then worked as a film publicist. Her award-winning distribution company ARRAY (previously AFFRM) has undertaken more than 120 film and television campaigns for various acclaimed directors. It focuses on films made by people of colour and by women.

I grew up in Compton, Los Angeles, California. Most people would regard it as a rough neighbourhood but for me it was a beautiful place. I had an amazing childhood, surrounded by family and friends and happy times. I went to an all-girls Catholic school, and wore a grey wool skirt from first grade to twelfth grade – very fashionable! At the time I wished that I was in a school with boys but I look back now and realise that attending a single-sex school allowed me to focus on friendships, sisterhood and my studies, which was very important.

When I graduated from college, I got into film publicity. I loved film so I wanted to work around it, but I never thought that I could be the film-maker. Then I found myself on many sets, engaging in long conversations with film-makers, and I started to believe that I could do it, too. And so I gave it a try. That was really my film school – being around other film-makers, then just picking up a camera and going for it.

At that time I was practising art-making for the very first time. I didn't grow up around artists, and I don't come from a family of artists. I started with documentaries, because I thought it would be safe to start with something I knew. *This is the Life*, my very first film, chronicled a little-known arts scene that was thriving in the place where I was from. I was part of the hip-hop generation, really loving what the music was expressing. It felt like it was speaking to and for me. All the people in the scene I knew personally, so I was able to get some great interviews and great footage. It was a remarkable experience. I had people around me who really wanted me to succeed, so it was a warm experience and a good first effort – and from there I was hooked.

I like having a sense of independence and that comes from doing things for yourself and doing them well. I like to know all of the parts of the process. Writing, directing, producing, financing, distributing and publicising my own first films really gave me a grasp of the full film-making process and the craft of it. A lot of film-makers seem to think their job is finished when they call 'cut' but there's so much more that goes into connecting a film with its audience, and that's a part of it that I really, really enjoy.

> At the time I wished that I was in a school with boys but I look back now and realise that attending a single-sex school allowed me to focus on friendships, sisterhood and my studies, which was very important.

I financed *This is the Life* from pay cheque to pay cheque. I would get paid for publicising someone else's film and then I would put it into my own film. For my second film, *I Will Follow*, which was my first narrative film, I took the $50,000 I had been saving for a house and financed and green-lit my first movie. *I Will Follow* was championed by critic Roger Ebert, who got a lot of people to notice it. Then my next film, *Middle of Nowhere*, got into Sundance and from there I was up and running. **In the early parts** of making *Selma*, I didn't really believe it was going to happen, even as I was making it. My father is from Montgomery, Alabama, which is very close to Selma, so I knew the place itself because I'd visited so many times with my dad, going back to his birthplace. I felt like I really had a handle on what I wanted to tell about that time in history and so I just started telling the story. And before you know it, it was in theatres – it was a very quick turnaround. It was so fast that I really never had a chance to think, 'Oh my gosh, can I do this?' I just thought, 'I'm going to keep going until someone tells me to stop.'

I felt like I really had a handle on what I wanted to tell about that time in history and so I just started telling the story.

If I find collaborators whom I feel are like-minded, then I'm happy to do things together. But as a black woman film-maker – and there aren't many of us around – there isn't a lot of support. So instead of not doing something, I just figure out a way to do it without the support. As you start to create your own work, like-minded people come around you and you attract help and all the things that you need – but you can never attract those things if you're sitting still. You have to be moving and doing something in order to draw it all to you. So I always try to keep moving and keep creating. It's not easy – but it's not hard, either. It's not hard to say, 'I believe in myself.' It's not hard to do something every single day that gets you closer to the things that you want to achieve. It's sometimes challenging, but more than anything it's exhilarating and I just embrace it. Some days you fail, but at least you've tried. **The landscape has completely** changed from what it was when I first started my distribution company in 2010. We now have Netflix, Amazon, all of these platforms where you can stream. The traditional walls have all collapsed. It's an incredible time to be an artist, an incredible time to be a film-maker, especially for people who had been left out of the old model – women, people of colour. Now everything's open, so it's on us to figure out where we want to be, to insert ourselves into the process, create new paths, and I find it very exciting to think, 'I'm not going to continue knocking on that old door that doesn't open for me. I'm going to create my own door and walk through that.'

Work without permission. So many of us work from a permission–based place and we don't even know it.

I always say the same thing – work without permission. So many of us work from a permission-based place and we don't even know it. We're waiting for someone to say it's OK, waiting for someone to give us a green light, give us money, tell us how to do it, shepherd us through. Some people get lucky, but most of us have to do it for ourselves, and the sooner you realise that, the sooner you step out and begin. Just begin and you will start to find your momentum. That's a very simple piece of advice, but so often I hear people asking, 'How do I get started, how do I do this?' You just start. It won't be perfect. It'll be messy and it'll be hard, but you're doing something and you're on your way.

Ava's Object
My journal. When I began practising reflection daily, my faith and focus expanded in a beautiful way.

LUCY BRONZE

Footballer and 2015
World Cup medallist

LUCY BRONZE

Footballer Lucy Bronze plays for the England national squad, and for Manchester City Women in the Football Association Women's Super League, the highest league of women's football in England. In 2014, she won the Professional Footballers' Association Women's Players' Player of the Year Award. Primarily a right back, she can play in a variety of defensive and midfield positions and has represented England at every level, from the Under-17s to international matches. She played for England at Euro 2013, and was acknowledged as the star of the tournament in the 2015 Women's World Cup, where the team, known as the Lionesses, achieved third place – the best performance by a senior England side since the men's team won the World Cup in 1966.

My brother's just under two years older than I am and I adored him. He loved football and I loved what he loved. I started kicking a ball as soon as I could walk. My parents didn't ever push me. They simply said, 'Do what you want, play sport, be active,' and I played all kinds of sports – I was good at tennis, but I didn't like playing on my own. I liked being in a team.

I was the only girl who played football in my entire region – rural north Northumberland. I played with the boys, and I'd never seen another girl playing football, let alone played against another girl. At the time, you weren't allowed to play in a mixed team once you turned 12, so the FA wanted to ban me from the boys' team. My mum and dad didn't know a lot about football at first, but by then I'd decided that I loved it. Football was what I wanted, and my mum got so headstrong when someone told me I couldn't do it because I was a girl – and so did my grandmother and my aunt, all strong, powerful women. My mum wrote to the FA and my aunt got in touch with lawyers. It was a case of you can't say that to my daughter, or my granddaughter, or my niece. [In 2014, the Football Association, the governing body of English football, voted unanimously to raise the age limit of mixed teams to 16.]

When the FA said I couldn't play any more, that was the turning point for my mum. She has probably been the biggest influence in getting me to where I want to be. In terms of what she's done for me, I don't think I could have asked for more. My coach said to her, 'You need to make sure Lucy keeps playing because she'll play for England.' I was 11 and he'd never said anything like that before. I didn't feel like anything special, but my mum and dad did everything they could to help me succeed. They drove me all over the country and, after that, I played with girls. Since then, every coach has said the same thing as my first one. Mum didn't realise how good I was and nor did I, because I hadn't had anyone to compare myself with. Once I started playing with girls, it was easier to see my standard.

I've been proud of lots of different things but 2015, the year of the World Cup, was a really big one for me. I've always been a good player, I'm consistent, I work hard, but I never really stood out until then. Before that, in England everyone knew who I was. Now people around the world know who I am. The World Cup was a huge highlight for me personally. It's changed my life in terms of perception and expectations.

To succeed at sport, the first thing is that it has to be something you love. If you don't have the love, you won't have the passion or the motivation.

There are 20 or 30 girls in the squad, of different ages, from different places, with different personalities. While we're all very competitive and driven, we tend to be quite caring as well – it's stereotypical of women, perhaps, but it's true. We all want to play, but we don't get too caught up in who actually plays – the team comes first. If someone's playing better than I am, I'd want them to be chosen for the match. I wouldn't want to let the team down.

To succeed at sport, the first thing is that it has to be something you love. If you don't have the love, you won't have the passion or the motivation. After that, you have to be driven – you really have to want it, and you have to focus. Ability-wise, I'm not the best, and I'm probably not the smartest, but if I push myself … The best players in the world, men and women, are so driven. Ability comes in handy but it's also about the hard work and motivation that comes with it. That's what all the England team has in some way, shape or form.

I think there's pressure put on girls when they're younger, so they want to be pretty little girls and look nice. Boys aren't scared to jump in mud and get dirty. The boys see male footballers, athletes and rugby players, and they don't care what they look like – they just want to win. When I was younger, I didn't really know about sportswomen. For me, tennis and athletics were the standout sports for women, and now we're seeing football, cricket and rugby, too. We need girls to play at a high level to act as role models for those coming up. My generation is doing that. The girls who are ten years younger than us have far more accessible role models than we had.

Football is the biggest sport in the UK and it's loved worldwide, but what girls see is men playing. Once you do tap into the women's side of it, though, you find that loads of women are playing.

There is progress but it still doesn't compare to male sports – there have been male footballers on television since there's been television, but females only for the past few years. Football is the biggest sport in the UK and it's loved worldwide, but what girls see is men playing. Once you do tap into the women's side of it, though, you find that loads of women are playing. Kelly Smith's always been a huge standout for me – an English player who has been the best in the world. She's set the bar up there, something to push for. She was the one and only female player I'd heard of when I started to look into women's football. To play for England before Kelly Smith retired was always a huge target for me, and I made it. I played four or five games with her.

To a certain extent, being passionate about something makes you a leader. I want to do well as an individual, I want the teams to do well, I want the sport to do well, so I talk about it a lot and I feel I'm a leader in that way. Things I'm involved with, I get quite passionate, and stubborn, about. I don't like people being negative about me, my teams or my sport and I will stick up for all of them.

I like to push myself. I'd hate to live my life regretting that I didn't do something that made me better, not just a player but as a person. If it turns out I'm not good enough, OK, I'm not good enough – but it gives me confidence knowing that I've done my best and couldn't have given any more.

Lucy's Object
A football. When you're playing football you're not thinking about anything else. You could have uni work, school work, you could be getting bullied at school, have family problems, anything at all; but when you're playing football, you're just thinking about the football. And any time I'm playing football, I'm enjoying myself!

CHRISTIANE AMANPOUR

*Chief international correspondent,
CNN, and host of* Amanpour

CHRISTIANE AMANPOUR

Christiane Amanpour is chief international correspondent for CNN and, since 2009, anchor of the network's award-winning nightly global affairs programme, *Amanpour*. Born in Iran, she graduated *summa cum laude* (with highest honor) from the University of Rhode Island with a BA in journalism. In 1983 she became an assistant on the international assignment desk at CNN's headquarters. She rose to become a reporter at the New York bureau and, later, one of the network's leading international correspondents. In the wake of the 9/11 attacks, she was the first to interview British prime minister Tony Blair, Pakistani president Pervez Musharraf and Afghan president Hamid Karzai. She also conducted an Emmy-winning interview with Libya's former leader Colonel Gaddafi, and Egypt's now-deposed president Hosni Mubarak. Currently based in London, Amanpour has been inducted into the Cable Hall of Fame and has been made commander of the Most Excellent Order of the British Empire by The Queen. She is a board member of the Committee to Protect Journalists, the Centre for Public Integrity and the International Women's Media Foundation.

I grew up in Tehran during the 60s and 70s. I have an Iranian father and an English mother, and am the oldest of four sisters. My mother was a stay-at-home mum – what we now call a chief household officer – and my dad was in the airline industry. Despite growing up in the Islamic world, I never suffered any gender bias and I was never given the impression that, as a woman, there was anything off limits to me. When I was young, I read a book by Italian journalist Oriana Fallaci, *Interview with History*, which collected her interviews with everybody from Yasser Arafat to the Shah of Iran, the prime minister of Israel, Golda Meir, and Henry Kissinger. I found it fascinating but I hadn't really thought about being a journalist; I always thought I would be a doctor because I was very good at the sciences.

As a teenager, I lived in a very privileged, cotton-wrapped, upper-middle-class environment, under a monarchy, and politics didn't cross my threshold. Then I witnessed the revolution in Iran, which had dramatic and negative consequences for my family, friends and country. I was deeply affected by the blood bath that happened after the revolution in 1979. People I had grown up with – friends of my father – were executed. I was being told that everything they did was evil and I was expected to readjust my worldview. Instead, it was the beginning of my

political awareness and I decided to go into journalism. I have spent almost the last four decades not only struggling to understand the revolution, but also all the other world crises that I have reported on since then.

When I started as a foreign correspondent, I covered the tail end of the fall of communism in Eastern Europe. My first big story as a foreign correspondent was the Gulf War of 1990/91, and then I covered Bosnia, which was a very different war. The Gulf War was a massive, US-led coalition to drive back an invader – Saddam Hussein, who had invaded Kuwait. Then, immediately after, I went to the Balkans – first Croatia and then Bosnia – and was flung into the kind of war that we see today, which is militias or governments attacking civilians. So that led to my reporting on the human condition in crisis. I am proud of my stories from Bosnia because I believe that we moved the dial by relentlessly telling the story of ethnic cleansing and genocide against men, women and children in cities such as Sarajevo and Srebrenica. Later, one of the most important interviews I ever did was with the president of Iran, Mohammad Khatami, in 1998. It was his first interview and many said that it was his manifesto for change and reform, and a game-changing moment in Iranian and global history.

I grew up at the time when Iran was a very

tolerant, multi-ethnic environment. While the majority of Iranians are Shiite Muslims, under the Shah there was also a thriving Christian community and a thriving Jewish community, and Iran had great relations with Israel. In my mixed-religion and mixed-ethnic family, I learned the very fundamentals of tolerance and fairness and acceptance from a very young age. I never thought that life could be any different. Of course my parents – a Catholic and a Muslim – could get together; of course I could marry a Catholic, a Muslim, a Jew, an atheist or anybody else – it didn't matter. But, through my work, I have seen that, sadly, issues of race, religion and identity are more prevalent now than they were and, in my view, the world has regressed in that regard.

I never suffered any gender bias and I was never given the impression that, as a woman, there was anything off limits to me.

I've always been very lucky – I have a huge amount of ambition and energy and a massive work ethic, so I have got ahead. I believe in helping other women to do the same, whether through mentoring, advising or sharing experiences. I use my television programme to move equality along. I am constantly looking for stories about the advancement of feminism and female authority as a way to redress the imbalance. If I can, I choose women guests, whether they are government ministers, civil leaders, doctors, artists or entertainers. I believe we have to help open everybody's eyes to the fact that we are 50 per cent or more of the population and that it is high time – and past time – that there was a basic level playing field. Much progress is being made – for example, in Saudi Arabia, for the first time in history, women have been allowed to vote and have been elected, albeit to municipal positions.

I would still like to interview the Queen of England, the Pope and Kim Jong-un of North Korea but, most of all, I want to devote the last useful working years of my life to pushing the ball of feminism forward and to making a just world for all women; because until women are equal, it is not a fair world for men or boys, either.

Christiane's Object
A photograph of my son, Darius. I have a great picture of him when he was four. He's got his little arm around my neck and his head against mine. I'm grinning so widely and he's giving the camera a knowing smile as if to say, 'Yes, I know my mummy loves me.' I married late and I had my son in March 2000, when I was 42. I never thought I would have children and having Darius was a major turning point in my life. He's a fantastic, wonderful, amazing boy who also, I think, has an intrinsic sense of fairness – I've probably drummed it into him. When he was very little, we were at an arts and crafts fair in Vermont, and I bought a bunch of napkins with all these great sayings, and on one was written: 'Justice not just us', and I was constantly flinging it in his face – we still laugh about it now.
He's seen different parts of the world through my eyes. I've taken him on several reporting trips, and he knows that life is about more than just enriching oneself. I wouldn't be disappointed in anything he did because I have met bankers and corporate leaders who have a deep sense of moral value, and I believe that, whatever my son does, he will bring with it a sense of purpose that is higher than just self-enrichment and self-aggrandisement.

BRENDA BERKMAN

First NYC female firefighter

BRENDA BERKMAN

Brenda Berkman is a pioneering firefighter. Born in Asheville, North Carolina, in 1951, she studied history before qualifying as a lawyer. When, in 1977, new legislation forced the New York Fire Department to open up to women, she sat the entrance tests. After passing the written examination, she failed the physical and sued the fire department on the grounds that it had been altered specifically to exclude women and bore no relation to what was needed to do the job. When she won, she left her job as an attorney and went to work as a firefighter, staying for 25 years and being promoted to captain. She attended on 9/11. Berkman founded United Women Firefighters and was the first openly gay professional firefighter in the United States.

My mother couldn't believe it when I became a firefighter. I'd spent two years in grad school studying history and three years at law school and I was working as an attorney. That's what I gave up to do a job that required just a high-school diploma.

I was a law student, married, living in New York and working on cases with my father-in-law's firm. We represented women police officers who were suing the police for discrimination, and we were handling a case for the New York City firefighters. At that time women couldn't even apply. All the firefighters I knew loved their jobs, which you certainly can't say about lawyers.

I've always wanted to help people and that's what the fire department does — when people are at their most desperate, they call us. It doesn't matter if the call comes in the middle of the night, in a tsunami, or from a poor neighbourhood where no one speaks English — the firefighters go. So when the law changed to force the fire department to open its doors to women, I applied.

I trained for the physical examination like crazy, carrying my husband up and down the stairs, running, chopping wood.

I studied and trained. You have to know something about construction, building design, electricity, water — you never know what you're going to encounter. When I turned up to take the written exam, the men were quite hostile.

It's hard to perform when people think you're a nut. I'd always played sports, I'd run marathons and I worked out. I trained for the physical examination like crazy, carrying my husband up and down the stairs, running, chopping wood.

It was clear to me that my score wasn't being kept properly. They weren't crediting me. The exam had been changed and wasn't measuring actual physical abilities. Not one of the 90 women who showed up to take it passed.

I thought there had to be one woman in New York who was capable of being a firefighter. So I talked to Bella Abzug [the leading feminist activist] and to a lawyer at NYU, my law school, and we went to see the man who was in charge of examinations for the fire department. He laughed in our faces.

So I decided to file a lawsuit. That entailed testifying under oath that if I won I would quit practising the law and take the job; otherwise the case would have been thrown out. Five years after I took the exam, we proved that it was not job-related and about 40 of us entered the fire department's academy.

I knew that wasn't going to be the end of it and the harassment got worse. I had death threats. I was followed. The instructors were free to do whatever they could get away with to make the women quit or get injured or fail. Just a few of us graduated on time. In the firehouse, the torture started all over again. I had formed the United Women Firefighters and been elected president when I was still in the academy. They didn't like that I was advocating for women, they didn't like lawyers, they didn't like that I wasn't from New York and they thought I was Jewish because I was married to a Jewish man.

They ostracised me. They wouldn't eat with me, they drained my air tank, they messed with my protective gear. At the end of my probationary period they fired me and another woman, the two most physically fit in the whole group and the two who were most vocal. I had to fight another lawsuit but I was reinstated and got promoted.

They didn't like that I was advocating for women, they didn't like lawyers, they didn't like that I wasn't from New York.

Some of the men came to respect me and some changed their minds about me. If I had discovered I was not able to do the job, I would not have stayed a firefighter. But I loved it and I was inspired by those women police officers I'd worked with as a lawyer, by leading feminists and by the people I'd learned about in history who had struggled for social justice in the suffragettes or the civil rights movement. My parents, too, had always done things to help in the community, at church or volunteering at hospital.

As I got older I started to find that I was attracted to women. I am still very good friends with my ex-husband. I really like men. Initially, I was not willing to come out. I was already dealing with so much, simply as a woman. But to become a White House Fellow [a programme that takes leaders in their fields to Washington DC for a year as assistants to senior White House staff] I had to go through an investigation so I was out as a lesbian that year in DC and then when I came back I found I didn't need approval as much. Some people harassed me because of my sexual orientation but some people had harassed me because I was married to a Jewish guy.

Any firefighter who tells you they're not scared is not telling the truth. As you get older and you're in charge of people, you feel responsible, whether you're working that day or not; 9/11 was off the scale of all that. I honestly thought I was going to die and I was very anxious about the people who were with me. We'd gone from our homes with no equipment because it had been sent on the fire trucks. I got caught in the collapse of a 47-storey building at 5.20 in the afternoon – the third to go, which no one remembers. Living or dying was a matter of luck – who was working, in what area, who ran in what direction.

It was hard afterwards, because who knew women were there? There were still relatively few of us – only ten more in the New York City Fire Department than when I won in 1982 – so the odds were that none of us would be killed. But we were airbrushed from history. The narrative went back to the need to be saved by men.

I was sexually assaulted in the fire department. I lost friends who didn't want to be involved with someone so controversial. But I also made friends. I didn't become a firefighter to win a popularity contest. I did a job I loved for 25 years and I still mentor and advocate for women firefighters. I think I've been blessed.

Brenda's Object
My fire helmet. It's the first one I had, with my captain's badge on the front. A machine replicated the shape of your head and built the helmet exactly. There were no chinstraps then. It's got a big dent in it from when something hit me on the head, so it probably prevented me from being seriously injured. It's damaged but it keeps going and it represents to me the value of doing things that matter despite the dangers and the setbacks. I would never have believed, as a girl, that I was going to become a firefighter. It represents the struggles of my adult life. It's me.

LYNSEY ADDARIO

Photojournalist

LYNSEY ADDARIO

Lynsey Addario is an award-winning American photojournalist. She began taking photographs professionally in 1996, for the *Buenos Aires Herald*. In 2000, she travelled to Afghanistan to document life under the Taliban and she has since covered conflicts in Afghanistan, Iraq, Libya, Lebanon, Darfur, South Sudan and Congo. She has been kidnapped twice, in Iraq in 2004 and Libya in 2011. Her recent work includes reportage of Syrian refugees for the *New York Times* and maternal mortality in Sierra Leone for *Time*. Her bestselling memoir, *It's What I Do*, which chronicles her life as a photojournalist in the post-9/11 world, is due to become a Steven Spielberg movie starring Jennifer Lawrence.

When I was growing up, we didn't have many rules. I have three older sisters and my parents encouraged us all to experiment and be creative. They owned a busy hair salon in Connecticut and at home we had an open-door policy – I never knew who was going to be sitting in the kitchen when I came in from school. We met artists and people who lived on the margins of society, and it taught me not to be judgemental. For a journalist, that is an important lesson to learn early on.

I started photographing as a hobby when I was about 13, after my father gave me an old Nikon that a client had given him. When I was in high school, my mother's friend, who was a photographer, started teaching me how to print and develop. I went to the University of Wisconsin and studied international relations and Italian and, after I graduated, all I wanted to do was take photographs.

> *I wanted to cover the war in Iraq. I had started to feel that I had a lot to say, that I could teach people and provide policy-makers with information.*

I never intended to cover war. I was curious about people and cultures and, having begged for a job at the *Buenos Aires Herald* in Argentina, I used my camera as an excuse to travel Latin America. Eventually, in 2000, I moved to India and while I was living there,

I started working in Afghanistan when it was under the Taliban. I had heard about the conditions for women in that part of the world and I wanted to do a photo essay on what they thought. Then, after 9/11 happened, I was poised to cover Afghanistan. I had already made three trips there under the Taliban so, to me, it wasn't a terrifying place. I covered the fall of the Taliban in Kandahar and then, in 2003, I wanted to cover the war in Iraq. I had started to feel that I had a lot to say, that I could teach people and provide policy-makers with information. It became a responsibility.

> *I always use the women whom I photograph as a source of strength.*

I was kidnapped in Iraq after I had been covering the war for a year and a half. It was April 2004, and we were driving on a smugglers' route to Fallujah. The road was overrun by gun-toting insurgents, who had their faces wrapped and rockets on their backs. Everyone was pulled out of the car and we were taken and held at gunpoint for a day. They were trying to work out if we were part of the military occupation. In the end, we were able to convince them that we were journalists, and they let us go. The kidnapping was very difficult for my family. My mother was devastated and my father said, 'Please come home,' which I did for a bit. My parents realised that I was going back, though, and they didn't try to stop me. This work had become my life and my parents were selfless in their support of me.

The second kidnapping, in 2011, lasted for six days and I was pretty sure I was dead. We were on the front line in Libya and tensions were very high. The men who kidnapped us were Gaddafi loyalists and had been told, 'If you see journalists, kill them because they are all spies.' They were hateful – from the moment they took us, they beat us and threatened us with execution. One of the things about being captured is that you are completely powerless and you never know how long it's going to last, which is worse than the kidnapping itself.

As a journalist who has covered war for 15 years, I am aware of the risks when I go into a place. We were in Libya illegally – we snuck in without visas – and we were covering a war. In any war there is risk and, unfortunately, journalists have become targets. It was my choice to cover the uprising in Libya and I knew there was a chance I would get caught. I have spent my life photographing people who have survived horrific things – women who have been held captive and raped repeatedly in war. Luckily, I was spared rape and worse and, yes, it was terrifying, but I survived and our driver did not, so it is important to put what happened to me in perspective.

> *It was my choice to cover the uprising in Libya and I knew there was a chance I would get caught. I have spent my life photographing people who have survived horrific things – women who have been held captive and raped repeatedly in war.*

When I was pregnant with my son, Lukas, I continued to work in countries that had been rife with war, although there was no fighting going on when I was there. It was a decision that I made with my husband and I felt comfortable with it. People who say, 'You don't go to Gaza or Somalia when you're pregnant,' fail to realise that there are hundreds and thousands of women living and giving birth in those places. So why is it not okay for a white woman from Connecticut to work there while pregnant? I always use the women whom I photograph as a source of strength and in Darfur I saw women who were six months pregnant walking for miles to go about their work, and carrying 50 pounds [22 kilos] of firewood on their heads.

Lynsey's Object

My camera. It has enabled me to walk into intimate moments in people's lives around the world. Without it people would say, 'What the hell are you doing here?' With a camera, you have a reason. I have been a photographer since I was 21 and it's what I've built my life on, but I am not wedded to one particular model – it's just a tool to tell a story and I go through them very quickly. When I was kidnapped in Libya, they took everything, including the shoes on my feet. As we were being taken, I was trying to pull the discs out of my camera – I wanted what I had shot. Cameras can always be replaced, but images cannot.

Every image is emotional, such as my photograph of Staff Sergeant Larry Rougle being carried by his friends, which I took in Korengal Valley in Afghanistan. In 2007 we spent almost two months with these young soldiers and, at the end of a big operation, we were being airlifted off the side of a mountain when we were ambushed by the Taliban. Rougle was shot and killed, which was tragic on many levels. It was very sad to see someone who was so vibrant one minute and dead the next, and he symbolised the greater tragedy. One has to wonder what the hell Americans were doing there, giving their lives to such a futile war.

LIMOR FRIED

Electrical engineer and
founder, Adafruit

LIMOR FRIED

Engineer Limor Fried is the founder of do-it-yourself electronics company Adafruit. Limor began Adafruit in 2005 while she was still studying at the Massachusetts Institute of Technology. Her goal was to create the best place online for learning electronics, and to offer the best-designed products for makers of all ages and skill levels. The Adafruit factory in New York City now employs over 50 people and offers tools, equipment and electronics that Limor personally selects, tests and approves. The Adafruit YouTube channel is home to hundreds of unique open-source project tutorials. Limor is also known as Ladyada, and took that name in homage to Ada Lovelace. Lovelace, a mathematician born in 1815, worked on Charles Babbage's analytical engine, an early mechanical computer, and wrote the first algorithm. She is regarded as the first-ever computer programmer. Limor was named Entrepreneur of the Year in 2012 by *Entrepreneur* magazine and is a member of the NYC Industrial Business Advisory Council. In 2014 Adafruit was ranked 11 in the top 20 US manufacturing companies and top in New York on the Inc.5000 list of fastest growing private companies.

I'm a female engineer and I'm really interested in how I can get more young people, especially women and other under-represented groups, to learn engineering. We can do a lot to get those people to realise how cool it is to be an engineer, but not by beating them over the head with a textbook. The way to do it is to present engineering as relevant. Becky Stern [her colleague at Adafruit] is doing a lot of projects on wearable electronics. Every week on YouTube you can find out how to make things such as a dress that sparkles when you dance, a hat that reacts to music at a dance club and an umbrella that lights up when it's going to rain. They're really fun – and they're complicated electronics projects, presented for people who think they aren't that interested in electronics, but are interested in fashion. At New York Fashion Week [2015], Zac Posen had a special project using electronics from Adafruit. We try to do that for everything that young people are already into – fashion, sports, technology, dance, gaming.

I'm lucky to have parents and sisters who are very feminist. I expressed an interest in computers at a very young age and, at the time, that was weird, but they were totally fine about it. My parents said, 'You don't have to have a traditionally female-oriented career,

that's fine.' Initially, I wanted to design video games; then I got more and more interested in the deep theory. Today, every kid has a laptop, an iPad, a smartphone. People have a lot more experience of technology at a young age, but they don't necessarily know how it works. Back then, you had to do much more yourself. It wouldn't be unusual to open up your computer and start messing around with it.

The best way to teach somebody something is this. If you want people to build a boat, you teach them to long for the sea; you don't give them the task of building a boat.

Technology moves very fast and, to reach more people, it got kind of closed off. Nowadays, if you buy a laptop, you probably can't even change the battery. Five years ago that was unheard of. If you have an iPad, you can't put an app on it without going through the App Store. It's very safe and easy for the user, but it's getting harder to get creative with technology. The best way to teach somebody something is this. If you want people to build a boat, you teach them to long for the sea; you don't give them the task of building a boat. For technology, you give them a project that's so cool they will do whatever it takes to be able to do it. It's very sneaky!

Then you start to learn how to modify things. Think about learning to cook. When you first start to cook, it's terrifying. How do you boil water for spaghetti, what is a simmer, what is a full boil? When do I put the salt in? Olive oil or butter? When you make your first meal, if no one throws up, that's good. Then you move on and try lasagne. Then you think, 'I didn't want it with beef, I wanted it with turkey,' and that works, but when you try to swap ricotta with cream cheese, it doesn't work. That's exactly how it goes with engineering. You learn what's going to work and what won't.

When I started Adafruit, I was still in school, finishing my thesis. I was really bored with it, so I kept building projects for fun – a synthesiser, the Minty Boost [a small, powerful USB charger] – and I posted them on blogs. They got a lot of attention. Starting a company wasn't my goal, but I kept getting emails saying, 'We want to build these projects, can you sell us the parts?' and after a while I put a PayPal button up.

It's a challenge to start a company. I went in blindly, not thinking how hard it would be, but I've done it. We give everybody the opportunity to grow, half the directors are women, and we're always hiring people and giving them a chance. What I like about running a company is that I get to make those decisions. If I had a venture company or investors backing me, they'd say, 'This is too risky.' Running a company is scary but if it's your own company, you can run it how you want to, and all the things you hate about companies, you can choose not to do.

Adafruit is awesome. I enjoy going into the factory every day, working with amazing people, seeing them flourish. Everyone in the company gets along. At the end of meetings, tech companies normally have a bug report. We have a hug report, where people give a shout-out to someone who's helped them – covered their hours, helped them with a project. It's

really positive. Instead of creating a culture of backstabbing, if we all raise each other up, it's better for everyone. We invite people to come and see these weekly meetings and they go away saying, 'I'm going to do that in my company' – we're trying to create a viral model of not being crappy to each other.

I'm a leader, but I'm not the boss – the customers and the people I work with dictate what I do every day.

I'm a leader, but I'm not the boss – the customers and the people I work with dictate what I do every day. I've offloaded so much of my task to the people I work with but they still have to tell me what they need, and for the customers, it's my job to give them a good experience. My philosophy is that the DNA of the company flows from the leadership – the owner sets the culture. It's really important to set an example, because how the leader acts is how everyone is going to act.

Limor's Object
An unassembled Minty Boost charger kit – an unassembled one has more promise. What the kit represents to me is an experience that someone's going to have. They're going to learn something about engineering, electrical resistance, soldering circuit boards. Even if it's only a half-hour project, they have something they have built that has given them experience and knowledge. It's scary at first if you don't know anything about building electronics, but if you get over that fear and jump in, you can run with the project and move it forward – and that's what learning is all about.

SALLIE KRAWCHECK

Financial advisor for women,
CEO and co-founder of Ellevest

SALLIE KRAWCHECK

Sallie Krawcheck is the owner and chair of Ellevate, a global professional network for women, and CEO and co-founder of Ellevest, a soon-to-be-launched digital investment platform for women. She has held more senior roles than any other woman on Wall Street, beginning as a research analyst at Sanford C. Bernstein, rising to CEO, and following this with equally prestigious positions in other blue-chip companies – chair and CEO at Smith Barney, chief financial officer at Citi, chair and CEO at Citi Wealth Management, and CEO at Merrill Lynch Wealth Management, the largest wealth management business in the world. Ellevate supports businesswomen at all levels, from those starting out to those in senior positions, offering networking, learning and investment. A portion of the network's revenue is invested in the Pax Ellevate Global Women's Index Fund, the only mutual fund that invests in the top-rated companies in the world for advancing women.

It's hard to know at 18 what you will want to be doing at the age of 40. Sometimes it's a case of making an educated guess – in my case, a wild guess. My journalism degree helped me enormously, though. The essence of journalism can be having lots of facts, information, sources, and cutting through to what really matters. The writing skills transferred perfectly to being a Wall Street research analyst. I was the fastest typist on the planet, which was also helpful. I had the choice of writing for a newspaper or writing for Wall Street and I chose Wall Street partly because Wall Street mania was prevalent at the time. There were jobs for everybody and I thought, 'I'll do that.'

One reason why there are so few women in finance is because we tend to know few women in finance. It's not just that you can't see the door, you don't know where the door is – you don't even know there's a building. And once we know about it, it doesn't speak to us very much. We are as good at math as men – we know that. The challenge is that the industry doesn't present itself well. Young women perceive that the finance sector revolves around making money, scandal, gambling – and they go off to learn how to be, say, a paediatrician. I'd say finance is about helping families to live their lives, and pensioners to retire well. The industry has represented itself really badly as long as I've known it, but in fact there is a lot of purpose.

I firmly believe the businesses I was running were open to people from all sectors and backgrounds. However, the numbers on gender diversity in the US have not moved. If anything, they've gone backwards. I think that progress has been limited. I loved working on Wall Street. There was a straightforwardness to it, a sense of action, that I enjoyed for years. But Wall Street needs to be diverse and we need to provide a level playing field for everyone. We have a gender investing gap in this country – women do not invest like men do and you can't tell me that's not because of a gender gap in the industry.

In terms of women in business, we need to kiss the queen bee goodbye. We've had too many queen bees and I've been stung by them, as have my peers. I do get it. Historically, the research shows that if there was one woman at the table – and back then there probably was only one – you didn't want another woman to take your spot. My generation and the next one are rejecting that. The table can be bigger, we can get more chairs, and if there aren't enough chairs for us in corporate America, we can start our own businesses in a way we couldn't have done even five years ago.

The number-one thing is networking and Ellevate provides that platform for women to meet, in person and online, to exchange ideas that help us all. There's an incorrect view that if I'm mentoring, I'm investing my time and you're getting something out of me. In fact, I get more out of mentoring than I ever expected. And people do find it easier with individuals of their own gender – guys have been doing it forever.

For entrepreneurs, their network is a key determinate of success – for raising money, getting together a board of advisors, finding customers and clients, hiring, knowing what competitors are doing. Women in their 20s say to me they don't want to 'cheat', they want to do it on their own. That's astonishing! Relationships are what drives everything – not just business, but personal life. We learn at school that we have to play by the rules, do the hard work. You study hard for a multiple-choice test that's on Tuesday at 9am and you get your A grade. The workplace is not school. My big break came about when I was on the cover of *Fortune* magazine for being the last honest analyst. We had the right business plan, we did the right thing for our clients, we hadn't got caught up in the research scandal, so I had my A grade. Then I was asked to fill in at the last minute on a conference panel and I said I would do it if the woman running it would consider looking at our business and writing a story on it. They wrote the story and put me on the cover, and the lesson was making that relationship – and not playing by the rules.

I never looked too far ahead. I never thought, 'How will I do this when the kids are in kindergarten or in high school?' I just got on with it. I never would have used the word at the time, but I was always authentic about it. The idea of hiding that I had kids or acting like it wasn't hard never occurred to me. It can be a tough thing for women to navigate. The world still likes you to pretend that everything's perfect, but I have found being honest works much better.

Relationships are what drives everything – not just business, but personal life.

A bunch of things make a good leader. You have to be smart enough. You have to work hard enough. You have to love it. Those are the prerequisites. One thing I think about a great deal is that you have to have a vision, and sometimes I don't – I don't always know which way this industry is going. You have to have strong communication skills because, if you have that vision but nobody understands it, that's challenging. And you have to be risk-tolerant. That can be difficult for women. We tend to be quite risk-aware and leadership can mean sticking your neck out.

You might be a failure one day, but you can still be a success the next. You can fail and succeed every day.

Success and failure are viewed as end points, not a process. In fact, you might be a failure one day, but you can still be a success the next. You can fail and succeed every day. If I get fired from a job – which I have been! – I won't like it but it's OK. I will wake up next morning and I'll do it all again – and approach it with a sense of joy.

Sallie's Object

A guitar-shaped pin. It was my grandmother's and she gave it to me when I was about six. She passed away when I was in high school. It's not real gold – the 'gold' is peeling off it – and I don't wear it often because I'm nervous about losing it. My grandmother was so proud of me. She gave me unconditional love, and she believed in me. She was a professional woman, which was simply not done at the time in my home town in Carolina. My grandfather had a clothing store. She ran the women's department, he ran the men's, and they were true partners all their lives. She was my inspiration.

SISTER ROSEMARY NYIRUMBE

Director, Saint Monica Girls' Tailoring School

SISTER ROSEMARY NYIRUMBE

Sister Rosemary Nyirumbe is a Ugandan nun who has dedicated her life to helping women who were held captive by Joseph Kony, the leader of the Lord's Resistance Army, which fought government forces for over two decades. Sister Rosemary joined the Catholic order of the Sacred Heart of Jesus at 15 and trained as a midwife. Since 2001 she has been director of St Monica's, a vocational school for girls in Gulu, which has given refuge to more than 2,000 young women, many of whom were abducted, raped, tortured and even forced to kill members of their own family during their time in Kony's army. In 2013, Sister Rosemary's story was told in the documentary *Sewing Hope*, and the book of the same name.

My childhood in Uganda was very simple. My mother was a housewife and my dad was a carpenter. Now I think he must have been the best carpenter in town because he managed to send all of us to school – and there were eight of us! I grew up in a culture that prefers boys to girls in terms of education. My dad believed that you should not let girls study – we should marry and look after the family. But, even though she was not educated, my mum was a very strong woman. She pressed the point that all her children must go to school and she said, 'I will do everything to send my children to school, even if I have to sell all the clothes I have and walk naked.' And so everybody in my family is educated.

I was the seventh child, and the last girl born in the family. I am considered the baby and I received a lot of love and care and grew up in a very positive environment. When I was a teenager, I joined the order of the Sacred Heart of Jesus. My brothers didn't want me to go, but my parents said, 'Leave her to follow what she wants to do.' So I followed the call from God and found what I wanted to do in my life, which is to care for children and the vulnerable.

My family lived just at the Congo border and, when I was growing up, there were already a lot of problems in the Congo. I experienced running to safety with my parents and having to sleep in the bush. Throughout these experiences what I always kept in my mind, and can still recall, is the love and care that I felt from my family. The women at St Monica's have been through terrible atrocities and pain in their lives. A lot of them were abducted by the rebels of the Lord's Resistance Army when they were young and trained as child soldiers. They were made to fight and, not only that, these girls were also turned into wives for rebel commanders who were much older than they were. They were treated as sex slaves and many of them had children through rape. A good number of the young women who were not killed managed to escape and come back home. They came with their children, but the difficulty they faced was that their community was not ready to take them in and would not accept them, or treat them with joy.

The women at St Monica's have been through terrible atrocities and pain in their lives. A lot of them were abducted by the rebels of the Lord's Resistance Army when they were young and trained as child soldiers.

I looked at the situation of these women in towns around Gulu and I decided that we would open the school gates to them. I told them to come with their babies and children. These women needed someone who could love them and help them to love their children. Of course with no one to care for them and accept them, it was very easy for them to turn violent towards the children who had been the result of sexual violence. But we could teach them to love their babies. We offered the women love and they started loving their children.

Every year we take at least 200 girls and the majority are between the ages of 15 and 17. We not only take girls who have been child soldiers, we also support women who have dropped out of school because of the conflict in Uganda or who are disadvantaged for any reason. We do not tell them that they have to leave after a certain period. The time they stay with us depends on their situation. If you have a girl who has gone through a lot of trauma and we see that she needs a lot of care, we will keep her as long as necessary before she's ready to go. But, as a rule, we keep them from one to three years.

> *We not only take girls who have been child soldiers, we also support women who have dropped out of school because of the conflict in Uganda or who are disadvantaged for any reason.*

While they are at St Monica's we give them the dignity of supporting themselves through employment. So one day they can say, 'I am going to live by myself with my children,' because they have the skills to be economically self-sufficient. There are so many things they can do – they make purses, which are sold internationally, and we teach them agriculture and how to construct houses from plastic bottles.

> *I am not alone in these ambitions, when I work, I have others around me who understand what I am trying to do and we work together.*

I am committed to doing small things that can bring transformation in society, for as long as I am able. I always say that my prayers – and my cup of coffee – keep me going! I am not alone in these ambitions, when I work, I have others around me who understand what I am trying to do and we work together. In 2011 we

built a second school in Atiak. I am also setting up an orphan village, which consists of family-based homes for boys and girls. So a number of children will live in one house with one mother. I have already got five houses built and I hope to build five more and take in 80 children. Then I will build a primary school, which will also be open to the community, so that the children who are orphaned and disadvantaged will not feel that they are by themselves. They need to know that they are in a family and also in a society.

Mother Teresa is my role model. I look at what she has done and think, 'What a good person, I can do what she has done.' But there are a lot of people who have helped me on the way to becoming who I am – my mother especially has been very important in my life.

Sister Rosemary's Object

A bag [purse] made from pop-tabs. The pop-tab purse project is very significant in the process of rehabilitating the women at St Monica's. In 2012 I taught the girls how to make purses from pop-tabs. First I learned how to do it and then I started teaching them – and now they are much much better at it than I am! It is one of the practical skills that we want women to have, so that they can earn money for their families.
For me, the purse is significant because it is something beautiful that is made of pieces of trash – pop-tabs that people just discard. The women with whom I am working were once considered trash but, with their paid work, they gain dignity and can begin to come to terms with their suffering. They are literally stitching the purses and mending their broken lives.

NELL MERLINO

*Creator of Take Our Daughters
to Work Day*

NELL MERLINO

Nell Merlino grew up in Trenton, New Jersey, and is now based in New York. She began her career as a union activist. After that she set up her own communications business and has worked on various political campaigns, and on many projects that support women in business and leadership. These include Take Our Daughters to Work Day, which she created in 1993, and which has inspired millions of girls – and, since 2003, boys too. In 2006 Nell launched Make Mine a Million $ Business with Hilary Clinton to help women grow micro businesses to million dollar enterprises. She is also the founding chairwoman of the Personal BlackBox Trust, an organisation on a mission to unlock the value of people's personal data.

Women need their own money. I started out as a union organiser, helping women to get a better wage, so I was aware from the beginning of this need to have enough money so you are not dependent on anyone else. It became clear to me that the greatest opportunity for that kind of freedom was owning your own business. Starting in business makes it possible to live the life you want to lead. I am not interested in money for the sake of money – I am interested in freedom.

People are so afraid of making the wrong decision. You need to be guided by yourself and that involves trying things.

What this brings to mind is the importance of parents and teachers in helping girls to focus on what they are good at. Girls need to look at the careers, businesses and opportunities that exist around the things that they enjoy doing. Sometimes people know early on what they're going to do – I knew I was going to be an activist – but things can change, and that's important. People are so afraid of making the wrong decision. You need to be guided by yourself and that involves trying things, in school, in an internship, as a temp. Pay attention to how you feel and what turns you on intellectually. Look for things you might not necessarily have been aware of previously.

I have witnessed stunning progress for women in my lifetime, but I still see this hope, a wish, that somebody else is going to take care of things for us. As long as you have at the back of your mind that someone else is going to take care of you and provide what you're seeking, we're in trouble. You see the manifestation of this, for example, in how women prepare for their wedding as though it's the most important day in their lives. I got married late, and I'm delighted I got married, but that choice was never going to be the making of me.

Powerful social and cultural mores still exist, and how women survive and make their way in the world is often too closely tied to the person they're with, as opposed to their own selves. Girls need a real emphasis and value placed on figuring out who they are and what they are going to do, not how cute and beautiful they are – which, yes, we are! But it doesn't carry you far enough. You have to have some kind of internal strength, and from that you have to make a living, survive, thrive, look after other people if that's what you choose. But it's down to you.

You can have it all, as long as you don't do it all. This is the importance of having the wherewithal – it allows you to strike a balance. There will be years in your life when it's impossible to do everything – someone's sick, or there's a new baby. It's a fallacy to think you can move through those times without challenges, but, barring those times, you have consciously to set up your life so you are able to work in concert with other people – family, co-workers, community. You need to focus on the management of your time rather than asking,

'How am I going to do all this?' Find what works for you.

One of my kindergarten school reports said I was bossy and when I later met the teacher again, I said to her, 'You wrote on my report card that I was bossy. You were right. I'm now a boss and a leader.' When you're a leader, people listen to you. You see things and call them out and people are glad you did, because they were thinking the same thing. Then you keep working at it. With Take Our Daughters To Work, I knew it was going to be OK because everyone was talking about it, writing about it. After the first magazine article, we had 10,000 letters. So many people felt something was wrong, and girls needed to be seen in a different way. I'd seen something that I shared with a million people. The key to leadership is exposing parts of yourself and of your thinking that give other people permission to act.

When you're a leader, people listen to you. You see things and call them out and people are glad you did, because they were thinking the same thing.

The people who inspired me first and foremost were my parents. They were extraordinary leaders themselves, my father a politician, my mother in the arts. They were activists, so you could almost say I'm in the family business.

One of the women who stand out for me is Judith Jamison, who was out of the context of anything I'd previously seen in dance. My image of a ballet dancer was an emaciated Caucasian woman. Judith Jamison is very tall, very dark. That image is so strong for me because of being different – I've always been overweight so I thought I didn't fit in and that's tough for girls.

Then on days when I feel I can't do another thing, I think about what Hillary Clinton's doing. Gloria Steinem [feminist, social and political activist] is extraordinary, and all the women during the Watergate hearings. For the first time, we were seeing women who held elected office on television every day.

For the future, I would like women to realise the power of their own personal data. Digital natives have an opportunity to shape the world. We can now quantify our lives, all the work we do, including unpaid, at home. We have the opportunity to say, 'This is what we contribute to the economy and this is where we want to take it.' We never had the numbers before, and if we want to be driving the bus, these are the numbers we need.

What happens when women's voices aren't heard makes me want to be involved, to make sure we're heard and seen. We make up half the population, we have to speak up – and when we do, things change.

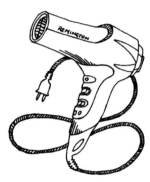

Nell's Object

A hair dryer. That's the object that immediately came to my mind, which really surprised me. We all need something that helps us to be our best selves. I don't think there's any leader who doesn't have some kind of practice or ritual before they go and do the things they do. If I've had my hair done before I go on stage, or on television, or into a meeting, I feel prepared, and I feel as if I've made an effort to present myself.

I've done an enormous amount of television talking about women and girls. I want to look the part of a leader and one of the things that helps is a hairdo. If you see a woman with screwy hair, that's all you remember when the point is to listen to what she says. If I know I'm going to look OK, I can concentrate on what I'm going to say. It's not vanity; it's being in the zone.

VIAN & DR DEELAN DAKHIL SAEED

*Yazidi member, Council of Representatives of Iraq
Doctor at the Sinjar Foundation for Human Development*

VIAN AND DR DEELAN DAKHIL SAEED

Vian Dakhil Saeed is a member of the Iraqi parliament and a representative of the Yazidi community, an ancient religion and culture of Iraq, centred on Sinjar in the north of the country. The Yazidi, frequent victims of persecution, are considered infidels by the Islamic militant group ISIS (also known as Islamic state or ISIL), and were brutally attacked by ISIS soldiers in August 2014. ISIS fighters systematically shot the Yazidi men; women and girls were kept alive as *malak yamiin* (spoils of war), kidnapped and enslaved. Immediately after the initial ISIS attack, Vian pleaded unsuccessfully in the Iraqi parliament for intervention; a week later she was badly injured during an aid mission when the helicopter she was travelling in was brought down by desperate Yazidi refugees attempting to escape their plight. The United Nations stated in March 2015 that the ISIS attacks on the Yazidis may constitute genocide. In 2014 Vian received the Anna Politkovskaya Award, which recognises women who defend human rights in conflict zones. On accepting the award, she said: 'It is a pleasure for anyone to be honoured with an award, but it is rare to see a Yazidi person who can feel happy from the bottom of their heart, due to the fact that our girls, women and children are in captivity as hostages of the most dangerous organisation in the world. I make no secret of the fact that I'm proud to be honoured with your esteemed award, but the real way to honour someone is by protecting their freedom and rights. It is by bringing our prisoners back.' She continues to campaign for the Yazidi people, despite personal danger; she has been called 'the woman most wanted by ISIS'. Asked about this at the 2015 Women in the World summit, she responded: 'I don't matter. It is nothing for me, because now I am not thinking about my life. I am thinking, "How can I help those people, those poor people? How can I help the minority in Iraq? How can I help the Yazidi in Iraq?" I do not think about my life. It is not important.' Vian's sister, Deelan, is a doctor and works in the refugee camps with girls who have managed to escape from ISIS captivity.

Deelan: A week after ISIS attacked my homeland, Sinjar, my father said we had to leave our home in Erbil city. I didn't want to leave; I didn't want to end my hopes and dreams there. We were terrified, children were crying and we had to escape and leave everything behind. It was the worst feeling I had ever felt – but I was among my family: my mother, my father, my sisters and brothers. What came into my mind were the innocent people forced out of their homeland after witnessing ISIS killing their fathers, assaulting their sisters and kidnapping their mothers – how did it feel to them? This changed my thoughts, my goals and my beliefs.

Vian: The Yazidi are a minority; we live in Iraq, this is our land. The Yazidi religion is a very old religion, from 5,000 years ago, before Christian, before Judaism, before Islam. It's not a part of any of those religions. On 3 August 2014, ISIS attacked Yazidi villages in Sinjar, killed all the men, kidnapped the women and killed their children. The Yazidi community ran away towards the Sinjar mountain; now 420,000 Yazidi people, 90 per cent of the Yazidi community, are refugees, living in tents and camps. There is not enough food, not enough water, there are no healthcare centres, no schools for the children. The Kurdistan region is helping people to escape ISIS, but we still have 3,000 people, almost all of them women and girls, who have been kidnapped by ISIS. More than 1,000 children aged between three and 10 have been taken by ISIS, separated from their families, and kept in special schools where they are taught to fight and made to convert to Islam. We are afraid for the future of those children as I think they will become a new generation of ISIS terrorists.

When you don't feel you are alone, it gives you more strength ... All these girls are our sisters and daughters.

Deelan: I work with girls who have managed to escape from ISIS captivity so I witness a lot of heartbreaking stories. These girls have suffered so much. ISIS soldiers are torturing and assaulting them. I witness a lot of physical injuries, not only psychological. And there is psychological destruction. From the start, when ISIS started to take the girls and women, they separated them from their families, and kept them in big halls and in schools. The soldiers separated the virgin girls from the married girls. They started by assaulting only the virgin girls, and after that they started selling those girls between themselves. The girls have a lot of issues and problems. They feel shame, it's like a stigma to them. One of the best things we have witnessed in the community is that families welcome back their girls (who manage to escape) and make them feel they should not be ashamed. They have been taking care of them, of their emotions and feelings, and most of the girls who have managed to escape have since got married.

Vian: I am asking the Iraqi parliament and government to help the escaped girls and to help the Yazidi community but unfortunately no one has helped them until now. Many organisations in Iraq, especially in the Kurdistan region, are helping refugees in general, but it's not enough. When we asked the UN for more help, now we have about 4,000 families living on the road because we don't have enough camps or tents, they said 'We don't have money to give more.'

Deelan: [The refugees] are in a safe region but they have nothing. They don't have money, they don't have jobs, they don't have any source of funding to rebuild their own community. They are living in camps so they can't build houses. It's a whole community destroyed. Maybe if some day we defeat ISIS, they can go back to their homeland and rebuild their community, with international help.

Vian: Until now nobody has helped these girls, but they can help if they want – they can. I am speaking about the international community, as well as the Iraqi government: if they work together they can defeat ISIS and liberate those girls.

Deelan: My mother was always the biggest influence in my life. She sacrificed herself to make me the person I am now. She was understanding and encouraging, and supported me the whole way. But my courage comes from my people. I was taught courage by a five-year-old child who had to walk for three days without food or water to survive. I was taught courage by each girl I sat with as I heard her story. I never saw the girls as victims: I saw heroes. Every time I had the chance to help them and saw their innocent smiles, I felt confident. And I never forget the people around me who believe in me, who never let me fight alone, and who support me. When you don't feel you are alone, it gives you more strength. I have adopted a 16-year-old girl who was sold five times from soldier to soldier. She has started going to school and studying and I wish her a better future. All these girls are our sisters and daughters. When I see all these girls with all these sad stories and I see such fear in their eyes, it gives me the strength to deliver their voices to the whole world. We cannot keep quiet. We have to tell the whole world.

Deelan's Object

I don't have an object so much as an objective, and the one that is precious for me is helping my people. Since I heard the first stories from the girls who have been assaulted and tortured, I felt those girls are my responsibility and I have to deliver their voices to the whole world. My objective is to deliver their message.

SHEILA NEVINS

Television producer and president,
HBO Documentary Films

SHEILA NEVINS

Sheila Nevins, president of HBO Documentary Films, was born in New York and studied to be an actress at Yale School of Drama. During the early 1970s, she began to work behind the camera, as a producer for CBS and ABC television stations. She went on to join HBO and has been head of the network's documentary production for 36 years. She has received 31 Primetime Emmy Awards, 34 News and Documentary Emmys and 40 Peabody Awards and, during her tenure, HBO documentaries have won 25 Academy Awards. Nevins's work includes the 1996 film *Paradise Lost: The Child Murders at Robin Hood Hills*, which exposed the wrongful conviction of three men known as the West Memphis Three and led to their release; *Real Sex*, a series about sexual trends; and the multipart project, *Addiction*, which was inspired by her son's struggle with substance abuse.

We didn't have any money and I had a rough childhood. My father worked in a post office and was also a bookie. Being a bookie in New York was against the law then, so we were always bailing him out. My mother had Raynaud's disease and scleroderma and, in her late 40s, she was wheelchair-bound because she'd had a leg amputation. She was a tough cookie. She had four brothers and she was the only one who went to college, where she majored in physics. My father wasn't home much and she was a hard mom. She wanted me to take over the world, to get As, to get into good schools, to be thin, to have long hair, to not pierce my ears – I did pierce my ears, but I didn't tell her.

It was the feminist Gloria Steinem who made me realise that I could be, at the very least, as good as a guy.

The need to earn a salary was the single most important factor in my life, because it made me want to be good at everything so that I could get a job. So if I didn't like calculus, I worked harder at calculus. I took the first job I could get. Nothing was ever beneath me – it still isn't!

I had an unsuccessful first marriage. I wanted to go to Europe and, in the 60s, a woman couldn't travel alone, so I married this guy from Yale Law School and, later, we wound up in Washington. I wanted to work in theatre but he wanted me to shop and cook and be home at night and on weekends, and I thought that was what I was supposed to do if I was married. The only daytime work I could think of that was close to theatre, was television. I got the part of a secretary in *Adventures in English*, programmes that were produced by the United States Information Agency and sent all over the world to teach people English.

I want to give ageing a kick in the ass. I want to keep doing what I do as well, if not better, than anybody else.

When I divorced, I came back to New York. I didn't want to be on camera any more, so I produced short pieces on subjects such as dog hotels for ABC News. Then I heard about a job at HBO, making this thing called 'documentary', which paid better than the job I had. Every job that I ever moved to paid more than the one before – that was the criterion rather than the job itself.

It was the feminist Gloria Steinem who made me realise that I could be, at the very least, as good as a guy; and that there was something inherent in the relationship between men and women that made it harder for women to succeed. Forty years ago there was a lot of flirting and laughing at things that I didn't think were funny just because some guy said them. I was pretty, skinny and tall and there were proposals and suggestions of infidelity that didn't interest me. The great advantage to ageing is that nobody pinches your ass – I don't know if men do that any more. They certainly don't do it to me! The nice thing about getting older is that people think you might have something to say. It kicks in with wrinkles, dental caps and bags under your eyes. People think, 'She must have something to say – she's still here!'

I am most proud of allowing anonymous people's voices to be heard, of making you care about a cause at dinner that you didn't know about at breakfast.

I am most proud of allowing anonymous people's voices to be heard, of making you care about a cause at dinner that you didn't know about at breakfast. I love the film *Paradise Lost*, and I'd like to be able to say that I made it to free three men – I did not. I saw a tiny article in the *New York Times* about ritualistic devil killing in Arkansas and my initial instincts were quite base – it was a good story and I thought I could get a rating. So I sent film-makers Joe Berlinger and Bruce Sinofsky down there and, after a few days, they called and said, 'We don't think these kids are devil worshippers. We think they're being framed.' So I said, 'Keep filming,' and then it became a cause.

There is always something that hurts somebody somewhere that needs to be told.

The *Addiction* project changed my life – and hopefully other people's lives, too. Before I made it, I thought addiction was a choice because I am not an addictive person (although I may be addicted to work). Then I saw that my son David was not responsible for his problems.

It was just as if he was diabetic or had polio. Everybody had said you were supposed to let somebody hit rock bottom and then they would either die or come back a new, improved person; but the project made my husband and I decide that saving David would be the focus of our lives, and I think we succeeded.

I won't retire. I want to give ageing a kick in the ass. I want to keep doing what I do as well, if not better, than anybody else. There is always something that hurts somebody somewhere that needs to be told, whether it's cancer or depression or homelessness, or the freedom to have a certain kind of sexuality or the right to be gay. There is always something that someone is getting beaten up for.

Sheila's Object

The little boxes containing my first, second and third dogs' ashes – Hamburger, Foxy and Corny. Euthanising Corny in 2005 was probably one of the hardest moments of my life. He got cancer and I had to give him up so that he didn't suffer. How I bury my dogs depends on how much money I am earning at the time, so the boxes are a sign of my success. Hamburger is in a wooden box, Foxy is in an urn and half Corny's ashes are in an expensive marble box and half are buried near the swimming pool where there is a plaque that says, 'If love could keep you alive, you would be here today.'

When I married for the second time, I kept my name and my own bank account. To this day, I'll say, 'That's my chair. I bought it,' or, 'That's my painting. I bought it.' I sound awful, but the distinction is clear in my mind – that I can afford to do something that I couldn't have done when I was younger.

CLARE SMYTH

*First female British chef to
hold and retain three Michelin stars*

CLARE SMYTH

Clare Smyth is the first female British chef to hold and retain three Michelin stars. Born in Northern Ireland, she grew up on a farm in County Antrim. The day after she left school at the age of 16, she moved to England to go to catering college in Portsmouth. After working in Australia, America and Monaco, she took up her current post as head chef at Restaurant Gordon Ramsay in Royal Hospital Road in London. She was awarded an MBE in 2013.

I knew from the age of 14 that I wanted to be a chef. Teenagers get very into things and I was very into food, but there wasn't much of a culinary scene in Northern Ireland. In the restaurant where I was working, the chefs came over from England, so I decided that was where I had to go. I always knew what kind of cooking I wanted to do, and I wanted to be world class. I was pretty headstrong and, looking back, I can see why my parents were worried about me setting off on my own at 16. But at that age you have no fear. It's only afterwards that you think you were naïve and stupid.

> *I was pretty headstrong and, looking back, I can see why my parents were worried about me setting off on my own at 16.*

I went to catering college in Portsmouth. Catering college doesn't really prepare you for working at the top of the industry, so I got an apprenticeship at Grayshott Hall [the hotel and spa restaurant in Hampshire] and worked there for four days a week as well. I had already read everything by all the top chefs, recipe books and other food writing. I'm quite an arty person and it's the creative side of food that appeals to me – the detail, glamour and beauty of it.

I love simple food too, but the kind of thing we do here, the creativity and plating, is a different thing. At home I'd never be able to cook in the way we do here at Royal Hospital Road. We have 18 chefs and 44 seats. It's quite rarefied. It's not just about eating. People come to have an extraordinary experience.

Once I had my qualification, I got a job at Bibendum in London, which was quite tough. I was 17 and I had no money, so I had to walk quite a long way to work. But I loved that restaurant. The produce they use is phenomenal. At that time I was the only female chef in the kitchen and I felt I had to be better than everyone else to prove myself. I couldn't ever say I was tired or that I'd cut myself, things that the guys were able to admit freely. I didn't think at the time that I was like that because I was different. It never really occurred to me that there was any barrier. I was tough on myself – needlessly, I now think – but that was mainly about doing a good job. If you do a good job, then everyone wants you on their team.

I joined some friends who were opening a hotel restaurant in Cornwall with an emphasis on Pacific Rim cooking, and then I went to Australia to immerse myself more deeply in that style of food. By the time I was 21 I was back in Cornwall at the same hotel, in Rock, as head chef, doing 60 or 70 covers, baking bread and changing the menu every day. After cooking at a couple more places – Michael Caines's restaurant at Gidleigh Park, and Heston Blumenthal's Fat Duck – I came here the first time round, to Royal Hospital Road, which had just won its third Michelin star. It was the very toughest kitchen I could find.

> *Some of the people here thought I'd last about a week. They weren't used to a girl coming into the kitchen.*

Initially, some of the people here thought I'd last about a week. They weren't used to a girl coming into the kitchen. In the past, girls hadn't lasted or they hadn't come at all. But in fact that period was pretty short-lived. Now women come in and thrive. I've got 7 women out of 18 in the kitchen here and this is one of the hardest kitchens in the UK, maybe even the world. Do women do things differently? Perhaps. We laugh and joke, but we get the job done.

I really wanted to cook at Alain Ducasse's Louis XV restaurant in Monaco but I couldn't speak French. So I lived in France for three months, having saved up to pay for tuition, and then I did an intensive one-month course in the language. It was exhausting to have to concentrate so hard, but communication is absolutely vital in a kitchen and a degree of fluency essential because everything goes on at a hundred miles an hour, people talking really fast in lots of different accents.

What really counts is to have the best team, which means everyone having the right attitude to work, with the professionalism and determination to do it well.

I was at Louis XV for 18 months. Alain Ducasse was a great influence because of his respect for the produce and the producers, his belief that the ingredients should be of the highest quality and reflect the locality. That means the producers have to be treated very seriously, and very well. The other big influence has been Gordon, for his work ethic, discipline and strong management.

I work 15 hours a day. I don't think it's a lot because in that time I can be doing many different things. In some periods of my life I've done 18-hour days. We have two services a day, which can mean up to nine hours. I pop up to Pétrus [Gordon Ramsay's modern French restaurant] most days. There are always tastings. I'm working with Gordon on opening a new restaurant in Bordeaux.

Restaurant kitchens are all about people and I really believe in looking after the team. Everyone's treated in the same way. You can learn technique but what really counts is to have the best team, which means everyone having the right attitude to work, with the professionalism and determination to do it well. The hours are long but we have weekends off and nowadays the staff have a night off during the week. Most of the senior team are married – I was one of the last ones, but I've just got married too – so work must be compatible with a personal life!

I have always had a fear of failure but, at the same time, I think you have to put yourself out there to fail.

I have always had a fear of failure but, at the same time, I think you have to put yourself out there to fail. Whenever I've gone into a kitchen, I have always wanted to be not just the best person at what I'm doing, but the best person they've *ever* had doing it.

Clare's Object
A little turning knife. It's tiny and there's barely any metal left on it. After I left the kitchen at Louis XV I went back for lunch a few weeks later. I'd left this knife – which had cost about £2 – and the sous chef had got it sharpened, wrapped it up in paper and string and put it in a vacuum package to present to me. It says a lot about him and the respect there was in that kitchen. Respect is really important to me. The knife has been with me all through my career. It stays in my little pot with spoons beside the pass. Everyone knows not to touch it. It's chef's.

MICHAELA DEPRINCE

Ballet dancer, grand sujet,
Dutch National Ballet

MICHAELA DEPRINCE

Michaela DePrince is a Sierra Leonean-American ballet dancer. Born Mabinty Bangura to a Muslim family, she was orphaned at the age of three and sent to an orphanage where the 'aunties' who cared for the children believed that her skin condition, vitiligo, was a curse and called her the 'devil's child'. In 1999, she and another girl from the orphanage were adopted by a Jewish American couple who had 11 children, 9 of them adopted. Inspired by a picture of a ballerina she had seen on a magazine cover in Sierra Leone, Michaela trained as a ballet dancer, winning a scholarship to study at the Jacqueline Kennedy Onassis School at the American Ballet Theatre. In 2013, she joined the Dutch National Ballet; in 2015, MGM acquired the film rights to the book she wrote with her mother about her life, *Taking Flight: From War Orphan to Star Ballerina*.

My uncle took me to the orphanage after my father was shot and my mother starved to death. He knew he'd never be able to get a bride price for me, because of my vitiligo. There were 27 children in the orphanage and we were numbered. Number 1 got the biggest portion of food and the best choice of clothes. Number 27 got the smallest portion of food and the leftover clothes. The aunties thought I was unlucky and evil because of my vitiligo. I was number 27.

I was always dirty. They used to braid my hair too tightly because they wanted me to be in pain and they told me I'd never be adopted. The only moments I was happy were because of my friend, who was also called Mabinty. We slept on the same mat and she used to sing to me and tell me stories when I couldn't sleep. She was number 26.

> *I was walking with this teacher one day when some rebels came towards us. A boy was following them and another truck full of them around the corner.*

I thought nothing good would ever happen to me and then, one day, I found a magazine outside the gate of the orphanage. On the cover was a picture of a ballerina in a tutu. I thought she was a fairy on her tippy toes in her beautiful pink costume. But what struck me most was that she looked so happy. I hadn't

been happy in a long time. I ripped off the picture and hid it in my underwear.

We had a teacher who came to give us English lessons and I showed it to her. She explained to me that the girl was a dancer. I was walking with this teacher one day when some rebels came towards us. A boy was following them and another truck full of them around the corner. They had been drinking, I think. They saw Teacher Sarah was pregnant and started betting whether she was having a girl or a boy. So then they thought they'd find out and they got their machetes and cut her open. Her baby was a girl. They killed her and my teacher in front of me. The small boy thought he should imitate the older ones and he cut my stomach.

Later, the rebels occupied the orphanage and threw us out. We walked across the border to Guinea. There were plans for most of us to be adopted, but not me. Finally, there was a plane to Ghana. I was miserable because I thought I would never see my best friend, number 26, again. Then a lady with blonde hair, which seemed amazing to me, and wearing bright red shoes grabbed my hand and my friend's hand too, and said, 'I'm your new momma.' Number 26 became my sister Mia.

When we got to the hotel, I started looking through my momma's luggage for my tutu and pointe shoes. I thought all Americans were doctors, models or ballerinas and she would have brought my clothes with her. I didn't speak English so the only way I could explain was to take the picture out of my underwear and show her. She understood straight away. She said I could dance if I wanted to.

When we got to America, I started going to ballet class once a week, then twice a week. I found a video of *The Nutcracker* and I must have watched it 150 times. I begged my mother to take me to a performance and I knew it so well that I could tell when they went wrong. By the time I was ten I was going to ballet classes five times a week.

I worried that my vitiligo would be a problem but my skin turned out to be an issue in a different way. A lot of people are still very traditional in their views and they want to see the same thing in the corps de ballet – white skinny dancers.

I worried that my vitiligo would be a problem but my skin turned out to be an issue in a different way. A lot of people are still very traditional in their views and they want to see the same thing in the corps de ballet – white skinny dancers. Early on, my mother was told by one of my ballet teachers, 'We don't put a lot of effort into the black girls. They all end up getting fat, with big boobs.'

I was stigmatised as a child and I had to grow up very fast. I couldn't show my emotions. Being adopted showed me that it was OK to be weak sometimes, that weakness can also be a kind of strength.

I have strengths as a dancer. I am muscular and I have strong legs. More importantly, I work very hard. I was lucky to be featured in the film *First Position*, which followed six dancers preparing for the Youth America Grand Prix, a competition for places at élite ballet schools. That helped me

to get a place at the Jacqueline Kennedy Onassis School and it also meant I was seen by different directors. The director of the junior company of the Dutch National Ballet knew of me. I spent a year there before joining the main company.

I was stigmatised as a child and I had to grow up very fast. I couldn't show my emotions. Being adopted showed me that it was OK to be weak sometimes, that weakness can also be a kind of strength. Dancing can be very painful and exhausting, which is why it's so important to have my family. My parents were able to convince me that all the people I love are not going to die and that, even when they do die, their love will always stay with me. They also made me see that it is OK to be different and to stand out. My sister Mia is a part of what I do every day and she and the rest of my family have helped me to appreciate a number of important things – it is possible for things to get better; it is a mistake to hold on to the past; you should laugh when you can; and you should look forward to the future.

Michaela's Object
A pair of silver earrings set with moonstones that belonged to my mother. She used to let me wear them on special occasions, and when I left home for the Netherlands, she gave them to me to keep. They were a gift from my father to my mother in the early years of their marriage. He bought them while on a business trip to the Netherlands. By passing them on to me, my mother made me feel truly loved and protected by both of my parents. Since earliest times, the moonstone has been considered an amulet for travellers and a path to wisdom. When I wear the earrings, I know they once dangled from my mother's ears. She is a very strong and wise person and I feel her strength and wisdom is transferred to me.

REBECCA ROOT

Actor

REBECCA ROOT

Rebecca Root was born a boy. She trained as an actor at Mountview Academy of Theatre Arts in London. When she was in her 30s, she adopted a female name and lived as a woman before having gender reassignment surgery. Her acting career has spanned television, film, theatre and radio. In 2015 she starred in the BBC series *Boy Meets Girl*, and became the first transgender actor to be cast in a lead transgender role in a mainstream UK sitcom. She received an Attitude Award for her performance. Root also appears in the film *The Danish Girl* with Eddie Redmayne. Alongside her acting career, she works as a voice and speech teacher, specialising in vocal adaptation for trans clients.

On one level my childhood was unhappy because I was living as a boy and I wanted to live as a girl, but on another level I just got on with stuff. I realised that my parents weren't going to let me live as a girl, not because they condemned it but because it just wasn't the done thing in the 1970s.

> *As I grew older, I understood that the comics and toys that I could play with were not the same as my sister's. I realised that there was a difference in male and female and I thought, 'I feel so wrong.'*

I wanted to live as a girl as soon as I was aware of anatomy, aged about three or four. I shared a bedroom with my older sister and she didn't have that thing that I had and I didn't have that thing that she had. And I wondered why. As I grew older, I understood that the comics and toys that I could play with were not the same as my sister's. I realised that there was a difference in male and female and I thought, 'I feel so wrong.' It was around the time when you realise that you write with one hand better than the other. I am not likening transgender to being left- or right-handed but it's one of those things that we have no real control over and, if you are forced to write with your right hand when you are left-handed, it feels wrong. It seems a crass analogy but I think it helps to simplify the nature of identifying with another gender.

I would like to think that my teenaged self – I am reluctant to say 'he', but I suppose since I was presenting as male, it's more convenient to say he – would be very proud that by being strong in the face of moments of enormous adversity and difficulty, I achieved my life goal to be the woman that I should have been. If I could give that teenager some advice I would say, 'Do exactly the same as you did but do it a bit sooner.' But that's life. Some people move very quickly in their transition, and others take time. I was in my 30s.

My parents love me unconditionally, as most parents do love their children. A prospective client was telling me about her parents, who are very anti her transition – they refuse to call her by her female name, don't permit her to come to the house dressed in female clothes and wearing make-up. My mum and dad were brilliant but it was hard for them. As well as my new name, they had to wrap their heads around things like when we were out, I went to the same toilet as my mum.

> *I'm not better than anybody else. I did it through sheer bloody-mindedness, because I refused to be beaten down or to give up.*

When you transition, there is a process akin to bereavement. But the nature of transitional bereavement is that the person you love is still here. I am still me. It's just aspects of me that you will not see any longer and some people find that incredibly sad. My previous voice was a big part of me. I used to do voice-overs and many people found it an attractive sound, but it was totally inappropriate for my female gender presentation, so I had an operation on my vocal chords to change it. My family knew I had to do it but felt a sense of loss. **Not every trans person** has gender reassignment surgery. It's not the be-all and end-all for some – but I wanted it and I had it. I was nervous, but it was just the kind of nervousness you have when approaching the first night of a play or your 40th birthday party. And of course I was asleep, so I didn't feel anything. Afterwards it was a bit of an anti-climax. Having the surgery was really just another thing that happened. For me, changing my name on 3 June 2003, when I was 34, was when I made my big statement to the world, because I was saying, 'This is who I am now.' That moment was when I achieved my femaleness. But I made that statement very early on in my transition, so I still had some facial hair and was looking a bit male.

When you transition, there is a process akin to bereavement. But the nature of transitional bereavement is that the person you love is still here. I am still me. It's just aspects of me that you will not see any longer and some people find that incredibly sad.

I am in a high-profile TV show and one of the few trans actors in the UK who is working at this level. I am not sure if that makes me a leader but it certainly gives me publicity and with that comes a sense that maybe I can inspire and say to anyone in a similar position, 'You know, anything's possible. Don't give up hope, because if I can do it, anybody can.' I'm not better than anybody else. I did it through sheer bloody-mindedness, because I refused to be beaten down or to give up.

As an actor I would love to work at the National Theatre and do more film, TV and radio. I would like to continue to help trans people to find a voice that works for them and suits how they present to the world. I would like to further the conversation that we are having in the UK about gender identity, gender presentation and gender fluidity, and to continue opening up people's hearts and minds to the knowledge that we are not freaks, we are not weird, we are just people who felt that they had to do something in their life to make themselves better. And the more people who see that, the less stigmatised my community will be.

Rebecca's Object
An ash tree in my local park. The roots form a natural armchair where I like to sit and feel the tree supporting me. It's not far from a well-used path, which makes me feel safe as, in the past, I've had stones thrown at me and once a guy attacked me with a dog-control device. I was early transition, so quite visible, and he took exception to my presence. He said that he didn't want his children coming to this park if there were going to be freaks like me there. He had a bulldog on a chain and it was snarling and the guy said, 'This is what I think of people like you,' and he started zapping this device at me. I was more shocked than physically injured but it was a very upsetting experience and the police logged it as a hate crime. I have lived in the area for 25 years and the ash tree has always been a place where I can go to seek strength and be calm, sad, happy or reflective. It's a totem for me.

TAVI GEVINSON

Editor-in-chief of Rookie *magazine,
actor and writer*

TAVI GEVINSON

Tavi Gevinson started her fashion blog Style Rookie in 2008 when she was 11. By the age of 13, she was sitting front row at fashion shows alongside Anna Wintour. She is the founder and editor-in-chief of *Rookie*, an online magazine primarily aimed at teenage girls, which she launched when she was 15. *Rookie* covers a wide variety of topics from a feminist perspective and is partly written by its readers. Tavi Gevinson was named one of the 25 most influential teens of 2014 by *Time* magazine. In 2014 she also starred in a critically acclaimed Broadway production *This Is Our Youth*.

I started my blog because my friend's older sister had one and I became aware of this community of young people posting pictures. It felt like it wasn't based on trends, or on gaining male approval, but on people who liked going to thrift shops to put outfits together. This was way before people could make a living out of fashion blogs – blogging wasn't something people were getting a lot of attention for at the time. My goal was never to be some witty kid on the internet who could be a source of amusement for a day. I just kept trying to chronicle the world that I was building, a community of people who, if we'd been at the same school, would have been friends. People talk about how the internet can make us less connected, but there is also that aspect of people who can't find connection to others elsewhere, whether that's at school or in marginalised communities. That goes well beyond my hobby, which is being interested in fashion, and is why, with *Rookie*, I want to create a place where people can make real friendships.

My mother is an artist and when I was little we were always making stuff so there was never any fear around creating different things – pictures, outfits – and it didn't feel a big deal for me to share them. Perhaps that's a part of being from a generation where everything is available instantly. I would get home from school, grab the tripod, go into the back yard and just do it. My parents were very supportive. They didn't know anything about fashion, but they were glad I was happy.

When I was 13, 14, the blog gave me access to a world that I would not otherwise have had access to. I lived in Oak Park, Illinois. No way

would I have been able to see a fashion show by one of my favourite designers otherwise. I found myself in a position to enter that fantasy world and meet people I'd admired, who turned out to be really solid friends and mentors. The Rodarte sisters [Kate and Laura Mulleavy, founders of the Rodarte label] were the first people in the industry who emailed me. I met them and got to work with them. They were – and remain – very concerned with turning the dreams that they have for their work into reality. All the other stuff is peripheral. I just want the freedom to do what I want!

I didn't mind if people didn't like my outfits, if people thought I looked weird. Fashion has a bad rap, about being shallow, about pleasing men, so I was happy I was wearing completely bizarre, unfashionable outfits.

I was OK with challenging people, making people uncomfortable. I didn't mind if people didn't like my outfits, if people thought I looked weird. Fashion has a bad rap, about being shallow, about pleasing men, so I was happy I was wearing completely bizarre, unfashionable outfits. People could see this was someone celebrating fashion – but not some beautiful, sexualised model.

On many of the fashion blogs I read, women talked about feminism freely. They removed the stigma around that word. For me, it wasn't that feminism didn't ever appeal, just that I didn't know a lot about it. It felt like a movement of the past, something out of history. What changed things for me was seeing the word used casually among people I thought were cool. With my outfits and stuff, I was already interested in challenging people, in finding other ways of thinking, and I realised I had been a feminist before I ever identified as one. **I was part of** this community of young people, making things we were excited about, finding each other, and I felt there wasn't much of a home base for us. I'd always loved putting together magazines – in fifth grade I put together a class newspaper – and, after a series of false starts, trying to get people to email me their stuff, I started talking on my blog about what an honest magazine for teen girls would look like. I had support from people who'd kept an eye on me, including Jane Pratt [founding editor of *Sassy* magazine]. An ad agency agreed to work for us before we'd even started, and well-known artists agreed to be interviewed.

I want readers to know they're already cool enough, smart enough, pretty enough.

There are people whose jobs are dedicated to figuring out how teenagers feel. I thought I'd go straight to the source, not so they could be targeted by marketing companies, but so that young people could have a network to find each other. Being online, *Rookie* has never had to be beholden to advertisers. There is no reason for us to promote anything that feels out of line with our mission. I think I've done my job if people are inspired or entertained or feel more OK with themselves after seeing something on *Rookie*. I want readers to know they're already cool enough, smart enough, pretty enough. It's about supporting contributors so they feel free to make things that reflect how they really are. Then more people feel encouraged, and hopefully more people can have the very positive experience that I've had, in finding others you connect to through your writing and your work.

We never tell people how to think or feel. We want to tell our readers that they already have all the answers. We want them to connect with the power they've always had in themselves, but possibly never knew about. If you want to do something, just do it! You have all the time in the world. You can start 80 new lives if you want. You have to try – and be open and excited about failure because it teaches you a lot.

My day is much better if I start out with writing. It lets me know I have something that's just mine – and it also gets me out of my own head.

The whole time I did my blog, I was also keeping journals. I wrote every day in high school, but didn't show anyone. Even if I had a lot to learn, there was enough going on inside of my head to put down on paper, things I cared about a lot. That felt like enough reason to have a place in these worlds I was exploring. Even now my day is much better if I start out with writing. It lets me know I have something that's just mine – and it also gets me out of my own head. You have to stay interested in the world and stay curious. Writing gives me confidence.

Tavi's Object
A necklace in the shape of a moon that was given to me by Stevie Nicks. One of her songs is 'Sisters of the Moon', and she gives these necklaces to different women she knows – it's this really special little secret. She gave me the necklace the first time I met her, backstage at a Fleetwood Mac show. I had talked about her in a TED Talk, summing up by saying, 'Just be Stevie Nicks,' and she invited me to the show and gave me the necklace. Her songs are so vulnerable and earnest and poetic, but so strong. She became so important to me in high school – and still is.

LAURENE POWELL JOBS

*Founder and president of
Emerson Collective*

LAURENE POWELL JOBS

Laurene Powell Jobs is the founder and president of Emerson Collective, an organisation committed to the ideal that everyone ought to have the chance to live to their full potential. Key Emerson Collective projects include improving US schools, advocating for immigration reform, and collaborating with partners who are creating innovative ways to improve social and economic mobility. In 1997, she founded College Track, which partners with disadvantaged high-school students for success in college. She holds a BA and a BSE from the University of Pennsylvania and an MBA from the Stanford Graduate School of Business, and began her career in investment banking before starting a natural foods company. She was married to the late Steve Jobs, co-founder of the Apple technology company.

I grew up in New Jersey, not far from New York City. I've worked since I was a young teenager, taking whatever jobs I could get — babysitting, lifeguarding, newspaper delivery. I left for college when I was 17 and returned to New York to work. After that I went to grad school in California, intending to go back to New York City after completing the course, but I never made it back. I met my husband, fell in love with him and fell in love with California. So after graduate school I started my own natural foods company. And several years after that, I was invited to speak to a group of high-school seniors. It changed my life.

These were high-school seniors who lived pretty proximate to me, but in a world apart. They wanted me to talk to them about college but very quickly I found out that almost none of the students that I was speaking to had taken the classes that allowed them even to apply to college.

I signed up to go in every week to meet with students and personally guide them through whatever process was available to them. Then I started meeting with teachers and administrators to talk about giving much more widespread support. Eventually, I sold my company and decided I would devote my life to opening up access to education for all students. That was the genesis of College Track.

Across the United States, the vast majority of families want their children to go to college and the students want this for themselves. But when you're the first in your family, and if you're a recent immigrant, or if you live in a community where you don't know anyone who's been to college, it's very difficult to get the information that you need. So that's what we do at College Track. We support students who are the first in their family to go to college, and we support their families as well. We focus first and fore-most on academic preparedness, but we also focus on social and emotional readiness, so that when students exit high school, they have a sense of self and a sense of confidence and purpose.

It's so exciting to be part of the removal of obstacles for students who have so much promise, so much brilliance, and often don't have any opportunity to express it. There's nothing in the world like seeing someone's life change. Every year I serve as a college advisor to high-school seniors. I get very close with them and typically continue that relationship through college and then through grad school or their first jobs. It's just so beautiful to watch a young person who is full of vision and aspiration start to achieve some of their dreams.

At Emerson Collective, we all feel deeply fortunate to do the work that we do. We spend a lot of time in the field, we speak to people in communities, we think about obstacles with others in our network — that is, people in government and business — and civic leaders. We bring people together around a common goal. We get to be creative and we get to innovate. We don't have to take systems and structures for granted. They're not calcified and inflexible — things can be changed. It's a rare privilege to realise that through our ideas, actions and work we can be a catalyst for change for the better in people's lives.

One of our principles at Emerson, following the transcendentalists and [Ralph Waldo] Emerson himself, is the notion of self-reliance and self-determination, but you can't have that unless you have access to the means by which you can rely on yourself – a healthy community, high-quality education, access to healthy food and clean water, and the kind of systems that allow an individual to reach his or her dreams.

We're working on a big project called XQ: The Super School Project. It's no surprise to any adult that high schools need to change. They're exactly the same as they were when every single adult went to school. Nothing else in life has remained static for the past hundred years the way schools have. We have to remind people of all the changes that happened in the world while schools stayed frozen in time.

> *We don't have to take systems and structures for granted. They're not calcified and inflexible – things can be changed.*

In September 2015, in partnership with the Entertainment Industry Foundation, we launched a national challenge for communities across America to redesign and rethink high school. We want communities to come together, get rooted in the student experience, really understand what students want in their lives, listen to them, interview them. All of the teams that have assembled across America have gone through 13 modules that we published online. In the process, they have learned about brain science, new teaching and learning techniques, and what new workforce demands are, and they've come up with very big ideas to change completely the high schools in their communities. Every single state put teams together. We have been overwhelmed, in the best way, with the response. It's way beyond our wildest dreams.

All of us who work at Emerson have worked in communities – I've worked in College Track

communities for almost 20 years – and we understand how knowledgeable, but generally how untapped, the thinkers and leaders are within communities. So we had a notion that, if we started at community level, and at community level they started by listening to students, and then architecting around that, we would get something special. And it's happening. It's really exciting to be in the middle of it.

Emerson Collective is still in early days. We're looking at what can we accomplish in the next 20 years; we're looking at all the structures and systems that contribute to inequality in America. The XQ challenge is a prime example – by galvanising communities to create solutions, we can ignite a new set of system-wide priorities to transform high schools to become far more innovative and effective for students.

We're also seeing lots of opportunity around immigration and in some of the other justice work that we're doing. Our objective is long-term, sustained systemic change, in systems and in opportunities, to make things much more equal, much more efficient for everyone. The best legacy I could have is not one that has my name on it, but one that has changed a whole host of lives because I tried to clear the path for individuals.

Laurene's Object

A statue of Ganesh [the Hindu god portrayed with the head of an elephant]. I have several. Some are really tiny, some are larger. Ganesh is the remover of obstacles, among other things. If I feel obstacles are too complex and too complicated and too hard, I always have a Ganesh there, on my bedside table or on my desk at work, to remind me that all obstacles can be removed.

SAMANTHA POWER

United States ambassador to the
United Nations

SAMANTHA POWER

Samantha Power is the 28th United States ambassador to the United Nations. She moved to the United States from Ireland when she was 9, becoming a US citizen at the age of 23. After graduating from Yale University, she began her career by covering the wars in the former Yugoslavia as a journalist. On her return to the US, she attended Harvard Law School, later developing a paper she wrote there into her first book, *A Problem from Hell: America and the Age of Genocide*, which won a Pulitzer Prize. Power worked as an academic in human rights and public policy before joining Senator Barack Obama's office as a foreign policy advisor. In January 2009 President Obama appointed her to the staff of the National Security Council, and in June 2013, he announced her nomination as US Ambassador to the United Nations.

I'm originally Irish. Both my parents are Irish and my mother came to the United States of America in 1979. The fact that my family was in Ireland, and I remain connected with them, certainly gave me an interest in events overseas. My mother is a medical doctor and so is my stepfather. I was directly inspired by the passion they put into their work and the compassion they showed their patients.

I had recently graduated from university when I opened the *New York Times* in 1992 and saw images out of Europe that I didn't think one could see in the 1990s – bone-thin, stick figures in camps in the former Yugoslavia. I wanted to go over and help, but I didn't have any skills. I had been a reporter in college – a sports reporter – so I decided to try my luck at being a war correspondent. It was a bit of a crazy idea, but a lot of young people were doing the same thing because they felt horrified and powerless. The journalistic community was remarkably easy to break into. Most of my best friends today are from that period. We were very tightknit, and we all wanted to do what we could to help.

I'm not great at languages, but I'm great at talking, and my stubborn desire to communicate with people got me to the point, eventually, where I could do interviews in the local language. When I came back, I wrote about my experience, and my way of doing that was not to write a memoir, but to look at the question of why the United States did what it did when faced with genocide in the 20th century. One key conclusion, after six years of research, was

how hard it was to make change. But it still felt as though no other organisation could make an impact like the US government. There were many examples of American action doing good – and occasions when it didn't – and it seemed to me that maybe it would be more efficient to be inside the government, trying to secure those better, more noble outcomes, than to be on the outside throwing darts at US officials, which had been my tendency.

Whether any of that would have translated into going into government had I not met Barack Obama, I'm not sure – but when I did meet him, I felt he was a real kindred spirit. When I started working with him, I had no thought in my mind that he would run for president!

Since I've been in my job, I've tried to inject individual stories into everything I do – real faces and real people.

I have always followed my gut professionally. I moved to the Balkans without a job and wound up as a war reporter; later I left law school to work on a book because the topic had seized me. These weren't steps forward on a conventional path, as my mother frequently pointed out. So my advice for young people would be not to decide on some title and try to script your path toward it, but to develop your interests, dig into them – go deep instead of wide. Learn something about something. I took a roundabout way, but I ended up inside the White House and ultimately inside the President's cabinet, advocating many of the same positions that I had advocated as a human rights activist and as a writer.

When I joined the administration, I found that, even with the best will, the crises and conflicts I had covered as a journalist were often reduced to abstract terms and concepts in the frequently mundane debates within the walls of the United Nations. So, since I've been in my job, I've tried to inject individual stories into everything I do – real faces and real people. When I chaired a meeting on Ebola as President of the Security Council, instead of having only the experts speak, we had a health worker from Liberia talk to us, via video conference, about having just had to turn away a father carrying his daughter, who was infected, because the clinic had no free beds. He described the father leaving his daughter on the side of the road because if he brought her home, he knew she would infect the rest of the family.

Empowering women to get involved in government and diplomacy does bring a different set of perspectives, which benefits everyone. This isn't a theory; it's a fact.

I'm not automatically for a particular set of values because I'm a woman, but empowering women to get involved in government and diplomacy does bring a different set of perspectives, which benefits everyone. This isn't a theory; it's a fact. The involvement of women in peace processes, for instance, tends to increase the likelihood that whatever plan is produced will hold. According to the UN, women's participation increases the probability of peace agreements lasting 15 years by 35 per cent.

I've had young children while I have been doing this job. My son was born in 2009 and my daughter in 2012. My way of making peace with this period is that I know I won't

be in the job forever and it's an opportunity to introduce my children to a magnificent global culture. I hope as a result they'll be more empathetic, more globally curious, than they might otherwise have been. My son is a big baseball fan, as am I, and he has committed me to something very robust. When I'm finished, we're going to travel around the United States and see a game in each of the different ballparks. I hope to make up for some of the lost time, spending more time in the playground than in the Security Council. That day will come. Life is about cycles, I think.

Samantha's Object
A framed political cartoon that I keep in my office. It has two panels, one atop the other. In the first, a man stands behind a podium that bears the UN logo, asking a crowd of assembled delegates, 'Who wants change?' All members of the audience have raised their hands enthusiastically. In the second panel, below, the same man behind the podium asks, 'Who wants to change?' Every member of the same audience looks down, avoiding eye contact. No hands are raised.

What I appreciate about this cartoon is how pointedly it delivers the message that if we really want to see bold action taken, we must first recognise what it requires of ourselves. As individuals, communities, or countries, we find it much easier to agree on the need for change than to change our own habits and practices. We hope change can come without sacrifice – who wouldn't? – but it rarely does. The cartoon is a daily reminder that in the pursuit of meaningful global – and national, and even personal – solutions, change starts with each of us.

97

JULIE BENTLEY

Chief executive, Girlguiding UK

JULIE BENTLEY

Julie Bentley is chief executive officer of Girlguiding. Since she joined the organisation in 2012, the Guides have become more visible and campaigning, with protests against sexual harrassment and calls for politicians to listen to girls' concerns. Julie Bentley has spent her career in the voluntary sector. In her previous job as the chief executive officer of the FPA (Family Planning Association), she fought to change the abortion laws in Northern Ireland, campaigned against a change in the time limit on abortions in the rest of the UK and argued for mandatory sex education in schools. She has also been chief executive officer of the Suzy Lamplugh Trust and worked in alcohol and drug services. She began her tenure at Girlguiding by declaring that it is 'the ultimate feminist organisation'.

I had no ambition when I was young. I was an incredibly shy and anxious child and not very academically bright. I hated studying and thought I was rubbish. I got three O Levels, in English, art and sociology. It was only when I got to around the age of 18 that I began to find my confidence. I'm not sure what changed. I'd been head girl at school – how that happened is a bit of a mystery, but I put myself forward because I felt it was important and because I was encouraged by others. The job involved raising money for charity and in that year I became interested in the not-for-profit sector. It opened my eyes to the idea of being a citizen and putting something back into society. I became interested in youth work when I was still a youth myself.

> *You spend most of your life at work and you need to know you're doing something worthwhile. We're put on the earth for a certain period of time and we have a choice how to use it.*

I worked for five years as a post lady. I'd get up at 4.30am, do seven hours tramping the streets delivering mail, go home and have an hour's sleep, then go out and start volunteering. I worked as a volunteer at a drop-in centre and on a drug and alcohol programme, and I did a huge amount to gain experience. That's where my belief in volunteering comes from. At the age of 24, I moved to London and worked in Bermondsey with people with drug and alcohol issues. I was doing outreach on the streets. The area was very difficult – completely different from how it is now. I worked with some fantastic but very challenged young people. I came from quite a nice little town in Essex, near Chelmsford, and it was a really formative experience to see the extent of the problems they faced, but also their spirit and potential.

The chief executive of that charity took a punt and employed me even though I didn't have any paid experience or qualifications. With her support, I did a diploma in counselling and then another one in management. I was ready to learn at that point, and what I was learning was something I could relate to real life. I did a part-time Open University degree while I was still working full-time and I studied for an MBA in my early 30s. By the time I left that job seven years later, I was the deputy director.

I think it's important for young people to realise that you can come from a non-academic family or a working-class background and still find your own way to success. You don't need to have been really clever at school. All you need is to be willing to work hard and apply yourself. It's never too late.

It caused a bit of a stir when I said Girlguiding was a feminist organisation but to me it's a no-brainer. For me, feminism is very straightforward. It means parity with men, politically, economically and socially, and Girlguiding has always been about encouraging equality for girls. It's a misconception that I'm trying to make it a feminist organisation. It already is.

I do think there are huge pressures on girls now, particularly as a result of social media. There's so much more stress on conforming. Young women are more exposed to stereotypes of female beauty than I ever was and we're seeing huge pressure to achieve academically. So much of girls' time can be focused on a need to be perfect. It detracts from being young. In our most recent survey of girls' attitudes we found that girls now are worrying about different things from those that occupied their parents – mental health, jobs and the future.

Young women are more exposed to stereotypes of female beauty than I ever was and we're seeing huge pressure to achieve academically.

One of the themes in my career has been working with and supporting women and girls. I am passionate about equality, fairness and people reaching their potential, about everybody contributing and being able to contribute. Girlguiding didn't seem like a radical departure. Its image belies the truth. People think I want to change it but, actually, I'm showing what it's really like. The organisation hasn't always been bold enough to shout about how fantastic it is – we've got more than half a million members, 30,000 groups of girls and young women meeting around the UK every week and a big waiting list.

Girlguiding is a wonderful combination of fun and the opportunity to develop life skills. We have a great badge programme. Our Free Being Me badge is for body confidence and helps girls as young as seven to unpack the images they see in the media. There's also our Be The Change campaign to promote advocacy and the power of using your voice.

I would never have imagined, when I was 16, that I'd be doing what I am now. If I could advise my younger self, I would tell her not to be so afraid, to believe in herself and her potential. I was very fortunate to have a good family. My mum worried about how shy I was and was constantly trying to reinforce me and build up my confidence. I was also lucky that in my first full-time paid job, I had a chief executive who pushed me to trust my instincts.

I made an active decision to commit to a career in the not-for-profit sector. You spend most of your life at work and you need to know you're doing something worthwhile. We're put on the earth for a certain period of time and we have a choice how to use it. I want to make the most positive contribution I can, and I believe that working with young people is a good way of doing that, because they are the future.

Julie's Object

A card from my mum, which she made for me just after I ran a marathon. I'd done the run for a cancer charity and she had terminal cancer and knew she didn't have long to live. She drew a star on the front in gold. The writing inside was her authentic voice. She said, 'Thank you for being such a courageous and generous person.' That was 13 years ago now and it's faded and dog-eared, but it's always on the wall in our kitchen and, if I am ever having a moment of doubt or lack of confidence, if the little Julie Bentley comes back, I look at it and I am reassured and encouraged.

LENA DUNHAM

*Actor, writer, director
and producer*

LENA DUNHAM

Lena Dunham was born in New York City. Her father and mother are artists. Dunham studied creative writing at Oberlin College in Ohio and made several short films. In 2010, she wrote and directed *Tiny Furniture*, a semi-autobiographical story, which won the South by Southwest Film Festival's best narrative feature award and caught the attention of Judd Apatow, the producer of Hollywood hits such as *Bridesmaids*. In 2012, at the age of 25, Dunham became famous when *Girls*, her television show about four 20-something women living in New York City, premiered on HBO; it is now in its fifth series. Dunham plays the main character, Hannah Horvath, and she is also the writer, executive producer and director. She has been nominated for eight Emmy awards and won two Golden Globes, including best actress, for her work on the series, and she was the first woman to win the Directors Guild of America award for directorial achievement in comedy. In 2014, Dunham published her essay collection, *Not That Kind of Girl: A Young Woman Tells You What She's Learned*, which went on to become a bestseller. The following year she launched, with Jenni Konner, a newsletter and website called *Lenny*, which focuses on feminism and politics. Dunham and Konner have launched the Lenny imprint with Random House, which will be a home for emerging voices in fiction and non-fiction.

When I was little, my mother told me that there are followers and there are leaders. That may be true in third grade, but in adulthood I think it is possible (and necessary) to be both at once. I follow and I lead, depending on what the situation requires. Following is relaxing, though. **I think a leader** is someone who listens, with compassion, to the needs and desires of people who have never been properly heard. Through this listening a leader gains power and can sensitively and passionately reach for what is right.

When I was young, I wanted to write stories that moved people and made them laugh. They could be poems, plays or articles in the school newspaper – I just wanted to use words to connect, to feel less alone. I also wanted a potbelly pig, which still hasn't happened, and I'm pissed!

If my teenaged self could see me now, she'd be like, 'What? You're dating a rock star! Lena, you DID it!' (She was mostly worried about boys.) If I could give some advice to my teenaged self, I would say, 'Sweet Lena, you don't need to fight so hard to get where you're going. It's happening without you. Don't flail all your limbs, don't gasp for air. Let the current carry you and just look around.' I think the expectations placed on young women by both social media and traditional media are painful and impossible to navigate, but I see a new generation fighting back and it gives me a lot of hope.

A leader is someone who listens, with compassion, to the needs and desires of people who have never been properly heard.

I want to use my platform [Lenny] not just to talk about some of the more abstract philosophical issues that women face, but to enact real changes to policy, so that other women in America, with less privilege than I had, have new structures in place to protect them. I want to change the rules. I also want to be a mother and, in whatever form I am blessed to have children, I want to give each of them what they need and to meet them where they are. I want to say, 'I see you.'

What am I passionate about? I am passionate

about women's rights, rescue dogs, wallpaper, cashmere, a good book of essays, New York real estate, rice pudding and genealogy. And what gives me confidence in myself? Eyebrow pencil. It really is that simple.

> *The expectations placed on young women by both social media and traditional media are painful and impossible to navigate, but I see a new generation fighting back and it gives me a lot of hope.*

Who is the most important person in my life? It's a tie between my mother, Laurie Simmons, and my creative partner, Jenni Konner. They are my muses and my co-conspirators and my loves. I'm also lucky enough to have an adorable and brilliant sister, a feminist father with a wicked sense of humour, and a boyfriend [American musician Jack Antonoff] whose support is almost dizzying. I must have done good in another life.

In addition to the women named above, I'd have to say Nora Ephron is the woman who has had the greatest influence on my life. She welcomed me into her heart in the last years of her life and showed me that I didn't have to be afraid of this industry or the men who populate it. She handed me my power on a delicate china plate. I miss her every day.

> *I also consider being female such a unique gift, such a sacred joy, in ways that run so deep I can't articulate them.*

I have been envious of male characteristics, if not the men themselves. I'm jealous of the ease with which they seem to inhabit their professional pursuits: the lack of apologising, of bending over backward to make sure the people around them are comfortable with what they're trying to do. The fact that they are so often free of the people-pleasing instincts I have considered to be a curse of my female existence. I have watched men order at dinner, ask for shitty wine and extra bread with confidence I could never muster, and thought, *What a treat that must be.* But I also consider being female such a unique gift, such a sacred joy, in ways that run so deep I can't articulate them. It's a special kind of privilege to be born into the body you wanted, to embrace the essence of your gender even as you recognise what you are up against. Even as you seek to redefine it.

> *When I am dying, looking back, it will be women that I regret having argued with, women I sought to impress, to understand, was tortured by.*

I know that when I am dying, looking back, it will be women that I regret having argued with, women I sought to impress, to understand, was tortured by. Women I wish to see again, to see them smile and laugh and say, *It was all as it should have been.*

Lena's Object
A drawing that my mother made when she was a small child. It's a group of women, dressed in their Sunday best, hanging out in a large empty room. The perspective is odd and childlike but the story it tells – that women are stronger in numbers, best in packs – is wise and eternal. Also I'm pretty impressed by my mother's kindergarten pencil skills. It was a big deal when my mother finally let me take the drawing to my house. She trusted me to protect something, not destroy it.

105

MICKALENE THOMAS

Artist

MICKALENE THOMAS

Mickalene Thomas is an artist, best known for her paintings made of rhinestones, acrylic and enamel. She also works in photography, collage, printmaking, sculpture and installation art. Born in Camden, New Jersey, she was raised by her mother, Sandra Bush, whose addiction to drugs when Mickalene was a teenager was one factor in the growing difficulties in their relationship. Another was Mickalene's sexuality. After high school, she moved to Portland, Oregon, to be close to a woman with whom she had fallen in love. She considered becoming a lawyer before switching to fine art, studying first at the Pratt Institute in Brooklyn, then taking her master's in fine art at Yale. Her work explores her own identity, sexuality and the relationship of women of colour to the world around them. It draws on art history and classical genres to question why women, especially black women, have been excluded or marginalised. Her work radiates sexuality, black femininity and power.

I had aspirations to be a lawyer, but while working as a legal-document clerk in a law firm, I had a growing awareness that it wasn't going to be right for me – and then I was invited by a friend to go on an art-therapy retreat. The plan was to support my friend rather than do something for myself, but it was a very important moment, almost like a calling. Everything fell into place. I couldn't have imagined becoming an artist but I made a lot of work – it just came out of me – and the response to that work was very positive. It made me consider going to art school.

My mother was an important figure in my art from the beginning. She was a very beautiful and sophisticated woman, whereas I was boyish and rough. I think I was not the daughter she wanted or had imagined. Naturally, as a parent, you have an idea for your kid, and, if you have an aversion to what they do, that's difficult. I was a woman-loving woman; I wasn't girly. I was all of these things that she didn't hope for. I didn't meet her aspirations for a daughter and, as a result, she felt diminished, because she thought I would be like her and I wasn't. It was not something she said, but something I felt.

I have a brother who is two years older than I am, and he and my mother were very close. I always felt like the outsider. It was difficult growing up and I think that made me more combative. My mother had drug problems from the period when I was in junior high school.

She met a guy who was a drug dealer and she fell in love with him and that just shifted my life.

Art has been a way for me to accept who my mother is and to see myself in her. It was also, later on, a way for us to communicate. Working together allowed us to get closer after we had been estranged. When she featured in my work and we made art together, we didn't have to sit down and talk, yet we could communicate how we felt for one another. Working with my mother was a way to reconcile a lot of issues we had without dredging them up and blaming each other. It was very emotionally powerful. The question we were addressing, perhaps, is how do you embrace the differences in an individual of whom you are a part, when that person is not necessarily the person you want her to be? Art enabled us to see ourselves and each other.

> *Working with my mother was a way to reconcile a lot of issues we had without dredging them up and blaming each other. It was very emotionally powerful.*

Your duty as an artist is to be something like a scientist, to find new formulas – to look at what came before in order to communicate a new way of seeing the world. You have to insert yourself into the ideologies of other times and other people. I am interested in claiming spaces that particular bodies – women's bodies, and especially black women's bodies, the bodies of women who love women – have no right to inhabit, spaces where we are supposed to stay on the periphery.

My art is an extension of who I am. It is trying to make sense of who I am and where I fit in, or don't – and if not, why not? I am working in film and photography a lot at the moment, exploring love between two black women – which, although it's part of my life, is something I hadn't put into my work up to this point.

> *My art is an extension of who I am. It is trying to make sense of who I am and where I fit in, or don't – and if not, why not?*

As a Buddhist, my mother was open to the world. She brought different types of people into our lives. She encouraged us to broaden our outlook, think about people of other ethnicities, consider different types of careers. I always had a desire to succeed and to see a wider world, and to question. I felt I had opportunity, a sense that there was more that I could learn, discover, experience.

My big ambition now is to have a building where you could have artists' residencies and where young people could go, especially young girls. I think it's amazing to be a young woman now. There are all kinds of role models and girls can think about becoming CEOs. It is wonderful to be able to imagine yourself in all these different positions in the world. In a sense, it is what I am trying to do in my art, to reimagine women in different spaces, through different eyes.

Even so, we are not investing enough in art and that has a constricting effect on people's opportunities – it narrows outlooks instead of widening them. Art is the first thing to be removed from poor communities when cuts have to be made, and yet it makes a huge difference to kids when they are able to be creative. It opens their minds and their imagination. A sense that the arts really

matter is much less prominent in education than it should be. Now that I have a daughter I think a lot about that. There are special programmes after school to explore the arts and creativity if you can afford them – but many of those who would benefit most can't. Then we wonder why young people become destructive and self-destructive. I believe that art saves lives. Period.

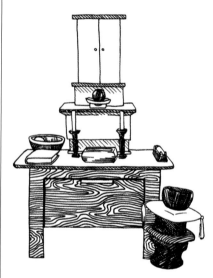

Mickalene's Object
The Buddhist altar that I have at home. I was raised as a Buddhist and although I wouldn't really consider myself a practitioner, it's the one belief I have veered towards throughout my life. I feel very strongly about incorporating meditation into my life because it helps to shift my focus back to my priorities, the things that are really important to me. The prayer altar is there to guide me in my daily practice. When things get too hectic and I feel distracted, it is a focal point of strength and comfort. I think of it almost as a 'refresh' button.
My mother introduced me to Buddhism when I was three years old. She was a devout Buddhist for 38 years until she died in 2012. We held an amazing Buddhist memorial for her, celebrating her life. I experienced first-hand how much she benefited from her beliefs. I see my practice as an extension of her within myself, and the altar serves as a reminder of the impact that she had on my life.

MHAIRI BLACK

*Member of Parliament for
the Scottish National Party*

MHAIRI BLACK

Mhairi Black is a Scottish National Party politician and MP for Paisley and Renfrewshire South. Born in Paisley, she studied politics and public policy at the University of Glasgow, gaining a first-class honours degree in 2015. She joined the SNP and campaigned for Scottish independence in the run-up to the 2014 referendum and then stood for parliament in the 2015 general election at the age of 20. She ousted the shadow foreign secretary Douglas Alexander from his previously safe Labour seat, becoming one of Britain's youngest MPs in history. On 14 July 2015, she made her maiden speech in the House of Commons. By the end of the day, the speech had won her 11 million online views and was trending in Nigeria. Her last job, before becoming a politician, was in a fish and chip shop. Black counts her passions as politics, music and Partick Thistle football club.

I was brought up in Paisley. It was Mum, Dad, my older brother and me. We used to go on caravan holidays up to the north of Scotland. My mum's mum had 13 children, so I had lots of cousins to play with. It was a good childhood. **Our family has always** been politically aware. My grandparents were involved in trade unions and Mum and Dad were teachers. They exposed us to politics. My parents were not knocking on doors during elections, but we went on CND marches. When I was eight, my parents, aunties, brother and I marched against the Iraq war in Glasgow. I remember my mum explaining that we were doing this because the prime minister was trying to take us to war, and we shouldn't be going to war. Tony Blair was in Glasgow for the Labour Party conference, but apparently he got word of the march so, by the time we were marching past the building, he'd already disappeared in a helicopter. I remember finding that really unfair, even at eight.

Inequality of any kind is the thing that really drives me. I always look at who's losing out and why.

Inequality of any kind is the thing that really drives me. I always look at who's losing out and why. Everything that I am interested in, be it foreign affairs or welfare reform or LGBT issues,

boils down to the fact that there's an injustice happening somewhere.

When I went to university, my course was music and public policy. I did music for my first year but I hated it – I love music but wasn't interested in the technical aspects. So I thought, 'Right, what other courses go with public policy?' I gave politics a bash and found that I loved it.

Mum and Dad taught my brother and me to have confidence in ourselves but never arrogance – there's a fine line between confidence and arrogance.

When the Scottish independence referendum was announced, I decided to start looking into things in order to make up my mind. I was definitely a 'yes' vote for independence and I thought, if there was ever a time to join a political party, it's now. So I joined the SNP and started campaigning. My immediate family were 'yes' voters, but my aunties and uncles were all Labour voters and dead-set 'nos'. I'm very happy to say that, one by one, I picked them off and they became 'yes' voters and, as far as I know, they all voted SNP in the general election as well!

I had no idea what I wanted to do after university and I had not thought of becoming an MP. But I have a habit of falling into things – whether it be university, politics or whatever it may be. I think it's good to try things and, if you're good at them, to keep going and see how far you get. Mum and Dad taught my brother and me to have confidence in ourselves but never arrogance – there's a fine line between confidence and arrogance. Confidence comes from giving yourself credit when it's due. I am passionate about football and when I was at primary school, I was one of the first girls to be in the football team. In fact, for a while, I was the only girl. My parents always said that as long as you know your stuff and you know what it is you're going for and why, and if you've practised hard and think you're good enough, then, by all means, stand up and make sure you're counted.

After we lost the referendum, a couple of folk in the local SNP party were saying that I should put my name forward to be a candidate, and I said, 'Don't be daft. I'm 20. What do I know about life?' I was giving myself the sort of criticism that other people give me now. People in the constituency, some of whom I really respect, started challenging me, saying, 'Why is that a bad thing? Surely parliament should represent everybody.' And I thought, 'Actually, that is a good point.'

I think part of the problem with politics has been people viewing it as a career. You shouldn't be in it in order to become first minister. You should be in it to try to do a good job.

So I thought, 'OK, I'll go through the vetting process and see if I pass.' I did and then I really had to think about whether I wanted to put my name forward or not. Mum and Dad spoke to me about it, and asked me a lot of tough questions – but ones that I was asking myself. I remember Dad saying, 'If you do this, you might win and that means that you're going to

be down in London a lot of the week. You need really to think about that.'

I've always thought that, no matter what job I ended up doing, it would be about working with people because that's what I enjoy – and I think I am not too bad at it. I'll be happy if, in five years' time, I can say, 'The place I am representing has been better represented than it ever was before.' I think part of the problem with politics has been people viewing it as a career. You shouldn't be in it in order to become first minister. You should be in it to try to do a good job. If you find one day that enough people are saying, 'I think you would be good at the job of first minister,' then that's a different story, but if you are involved in politics, it has to be for a purpose and it has to be in the present. If more people adhere to that, then politics will become healthier altogether.

Mhairi's Object
A bar of chocolate. When I was at primary school, I used to go with my mum to stay with my granny, who lived a 20-minute drive away. My uncle was severely physically and mentally disabled and we would help my granny to look after him. I was a terrible worrier when I was a child, and if I had a spelling test at school next day, I would be thinking, 'I don't know enough, I haven't worked hard enough.'

My granny used to give me a Galaxy bar for good luck. The tests were always in the morning so, by the time I got to eat the Galaxy, it was a victory chocolate bar. It became a thing and, after I won the election, I treated myself to a Galaxy!

JO MALONE

*Perfumer, entrepreneur
and founder, Jo Loves*

JO MALONE

Jo Malone, creator of some of the world's most popular fragrances, was raised in a council house in Kent. She left school with no qualifications and became a facial therapist, making scented products by hand in her kitchen. From these artisan beginnings, Malone launched her first luxury brand, Jo Malone London, with her husband Gary Willcox. In 1999 they sold the business to Estée Lauder Companies and Malone remained creative director until she left in 2006. Two years later she was awarded the MBE for her services to the beauty industry. In 2011, she unveiled her new brand, Jo Loves. A cancer survivor, Malone had a double mastectomy after she was diagnosed with an aggressive form of breast cancer in 2003.

I would have been happy with a tenth of my life. If someone had told me when I was teenager that I would go on to be happily married and have a business, I don't think I would have believed them – I would have sat with my mouth open!

By the time I was 12, I was the grown-up in our family a lot of the time. My dad, as wonderful as he was, was probably bi-polar – I think my mum was as well. Living with people displaying those characteristics was very difficult. When my mum and dad were doing well, they were the grown-ups and the fridge was full, but when they weren't, there was nothing in there and it was my responsibility to try to keep things on an even keel for my younger sister and me. To this day, on a Sunday night, we eat up whatever's in the fridge (we call it 'bits and pieces'), because bits and pieces were a luxury when I was a child. **It wasn't the easiest** childhood, but I wasn't unhappy and I had two very creative parents. My father was an artist and I would get up very early on Saturdays and Sundays to go to markets with him to help sell his paintings. That's where I cut my teeth in retail. My mum was a beautician. She used to leave me with a big enamel pot and the formula for her products and, after she'd shown me a few times, I could make them in the kitchen very quickly. Although we lived on a council estate, she had one smart outfit that she wore to work – an Yves Saint Laurent silk shirt, a beautiful Jaeger velvet skirt and high Rayne wedges. She would say, 'If you can have one thing, make sure that it's the best,' and that has stayed with me all my life.

I am dyslexic. I never took exams and I never finished school but dyslexia has been my best friend. Dyslexics often think outside the box because they can't do things in a conventional way. When I look at business problems, I always think of the less obvious solution. I create fragrance in the same way – always looking for the bit that's different. I am not a particularly confident person and when I'm feeling insecure, I run to my creative world, and that's often when I create my best things.

It wasn't the easiest childhood, but I wasn't unhappy and I had two very creative parents.

I became a skin-care therapist like my mum, and I used to make all my own treatments and little products, too. I had the products in my sitting room and people would come and buy. I remember someone in Singapore wanted 500 bags of potpourri, which were picked up and put on a private jet! Demand grew and when Gary and I were newly married, he said, 'How about a shop?' There was no way I wanted a shop, but he coaxed me round and we opened one in London in 1994. Scented candles went on to become one of the biggest parts of the Jo Malone brand. I made the first 12 by myself and they looked terrible but smelt amazing. So I found a factory to make the first 50, then the next 100 and the rest is history.

When I had cancer, I thought I was going to die. My main priority was to stay alive for my son Josh. I gave myself a year for surgery and treatment and then I had it in my mind that I wanted my life back – and I wanted it back just as it had been. At the end of my treatment, I was really messed up in my head from the whole thing. I went to see a brilliant psychologist, who said, 'You can't have your life back as it was, it's gone. But your life can be even better.'

When I had cancer, I thought I was going to die. My main priority was to stay alive for my son Josh.

I hated her for saying it but then, as the months went by, I realised that I quite liked the strength that I'd gathered over the year – but, when I tried to go back to the company, Jo Malone, I realised that I didn't fit in any more. So I walked away. I didn't know whether the cancer was going to return and I wanted to spend time with my son – taking him to and from school and going to sports day. As time went on I realised the cancer wasn't going to come back and I was left with this huge void. What I hadn't anticipated was the love affair that I had with fragrance.

As time went on I realised the cancer wasn't going to come back and I was left with this huge void. What I hadn't anticipated was the love affair that I had with fragrance.

When I walked away from my contract with Estée Lauder, what's called a 'lock out' was imposed, under which I was prevented, rightly so, from entering the industry again for five years. Those five years were excruciating. I made TV shows, I sat on boards, I did all sorts of things, but nothing made me feel whole again. All I really wanted to do was sit at the kitchen table with lots of bottles and create. So, in 2011, when I was clear of cancer and my

son had grown up, I decided to take the plunge and start again. I want to build another global brand and I am well on the way. At the minute all anyone sees is one little shop – but watch this space.

I have lots of strong women in my life that I love but the one person that I have walked round the world with is Charlotte McCarthy [Communications Director of Jo Loves]. Charlotte came to Jo Malone as an intern all those years ago so she knows me incredibly well. When things were tough in the company we stood side by side and carried on building, so I have a lot to thank her for. We get cross with each other but we're great friends and we adore each other. She's like my kid sister and it's lovely to have her in my life.

Jo's Object
My wooden kitchen table. It's French and it's where I have built a lot of my life. Not only have I had black-tie dinners with amazing people – I've fitted 14 at a squeeze – but I built the global brand Jo Malone round that table. It's where we've celebrated and it's where I sat and cried the day I was diagnosed with cancer. More recently, it's where Gary and I started Jo Loves. We could have had a smart office but we didn't go for that. We started at the kitchen table again with four computers.
We had a fire in our house a few years ago and the table was saved, thank goodness. It smelled of smoke but we rubbed it down and gave it a good polish, just as you do in life – you scrub up well and off you go again. The kitchen table will always be part of our lives and, if it could talk, it would tell an epic story.

ROYA MAHBOOB

*Technology entrepreneur and
co-founder, Digital Citizen Fund*

ROYA MAHBOOB

Technology entrepreneur Roya Mahboob was born in 1987 in Iran, where her family was exiled during the Soviet occupation of Afghanistan and the subsequent Taliban takeover, which precipitated the destruction of girls' schools across the country. Her family finally returned to Afghanistan in 2003, and Roya went on to gain a computer science degree from Herat University. In 2010 she co-founded a software company, Afghan Citadel, which won contracts with private companies, government ministries and NATO. She also co-founded Women's Annex Foundation (now Digital Citizen Fund), a non-profit organisation that seeks to increase digital literacy by the establishment of computer labs where women and girls learn to use social media and produce content for which they are paid. In 2013, beset with death threats, Roya was forced to move to America on an expedited visa. She has since formed a new company, EdyEdy, an online learning platform.

I was born a migrant. Before the Russians attacked Afghanistan, my father was an engineer and my mum worked for the government. My family left for Iran and I was born there. I loved to study and my father, who taught in a private university, used to take me with him to college. It made me want to be like him.

We have to educate women to teach their sons to respect their mothers and sisters and to allow their daughters to be educated.

In 2003 we went back to Afghanistan and I applied for Herat University. I was lucky because my family was educated and my mother had worked. My parents gave me the opportunity to do the same, but it wasn't the case for other girls. Most can't go to university. They marry and have children. They may have dreams of working but, because of tradition, it's not easy for them to do so. The Afghan people believe that women should stay at home and don't consider that they can participate in society. It's not just the fault of men; it's the fault of women, too. They allow it to happen. So we have to educate women to teach their sons to respect their mothers and sisters and to allow their daughters to be educated.

The education that I provide is not about reading and writing, it's about digital literacy. I

focus on that because it changed my life. I remember wanting to know what was going on in the world but we only had a TV. When I started to learn about the internet and to connect with social media, I became more confident and was so happy. Self-confidence is like magic because everything seems possible and, if you have skills, you can make things happen. For me, everything is like a challenge and I want to prove that I can do it, especially when I hear people say that, as a woman, I can't.

In 2010 I started Afghan Citadel Software Company with the aim of providing job opportunities for females. I also established IT centres – 11 located in schools – and we have educated almost 8,000 women and girls. Men in conservative societies often don't see women as first-class citizens but connectivity enables a woman to earn money, which can give her more status in the family. One such woman had been a student until she married and had children. Then she had the responsibility of the home, and her husband wouldn't pay for her university studies. She began writing articles for the Women's Annex Foundation and got paid well in Bitcoin. She bought a laptop and started a successful fashion business, which has made her very popular with her husband!

My mum was my greatest influence because she did not rely on my father. When they moved to Iran, she couldn't work, so she started making handicrafts, just to be independent. In terms of business, I look to Sheryl Sandberg – she is a millionaire, a successful leader and a successful mum. I read her book, *Lean In*, and I follow her practical advice.

I am a good leader because I am an innovator – I find solutions and make things happen. I don't just dream. I find which person is good for which job and try to manage problems. Social media not only plays a powerful role in my personal life, it also helps me to resolve business difficulties in an innovative way. I am persistent and an optimist, but I am also realistic and honest with my team, which is important. I haven't ever felt like giving up, but I have had to rethink or change direction to help women in a different way.

The problem is, as a woman, if you get famous in Afghanistan in any field, you put yourself in danger.

Herat is very conservative and, when I was building the company, people said very bad things about me and there were threats. My father supported me, as did my four brothers. The problem is, as a woman, if you get famous in Afghanistan in any field, you put yourself in danger. I featured in magazines and, while having my work recognised helped when I was finding people to support my projects, I couldn't stay low profile, and this created problem after problem. At the time, corruption was high and you couldn't trust anybody. The threats increased and it became dangerous for my employees as well as for me. I left Afghanistan because I thought, 'Everything is about me and if I am not here, they won't care so much about what is going on.'

Now, after two years away, I hope to go back. I trust this new government more than the previous one, which didn't support my work. I have a new platform called EdyEdy, which means Educate Yourself, and I am hoping that it will help every woman, not only in Afghanistan but in other countries as well. The idea is to provide education and access to job opportunities that are acceptable

to the culture. It doesn't matter if a family won't allow a woman to go to school or to work in an office, because the education and work is done online via cell phone, tablet or computer. Women can be connected with local or international companies that offer training with a job. They get paid at a lower rate while they gain experience and then, when they have graduated with a certificate, they can freelance for these companies and get paid more, either by PayPal or Bitcoin.

Through my foundation, Digital Citizen Fund, I want to build between 50 and 100 more IT centres in Afghanistan over the next five years and give connectivity to half a million female students, not only in the cities Kabul and Herat, but in country areas, too. Conservative society wants to keep women quiet. Connectivity is the best tool to raise our voices – they can't keep hundreds and thousands of women silent.

Roya's Object

A bird. I identify with a free bird, not one in a cage but one that can fly anywhere, with no limits. A bird is not linked to a country or a nation. It just flies. As a digital citizen using social media, there are no borders for me, and people don't discriminate against me because of my gender or nationality. My life is like that of a migrating bird. When I was a child, we went from Iran to Afghanistan and then back to Iran, finally returning to Herat in 2003. Two years ago, I had to move to the States where I had to start again from scratch. I have always felt like a migrant, but my heart is in Afghanistan and I am always connected via social media to my country.

TINA BROWN

Founder of Women in the World,
editor and author

TINA BROWN

Tina Brown is a journalist, editor and author. She went to Oxford at the age of 17, wrote for the university magazine and was published in the *New Statesman* while still an undergraduate. She won a National Student Drama Award for a play she wrote during her time at Oxford; the Bush Theatre staged a second. At the age of 25, she was appointed editor of *Tatler*; in 1984, she moved to New York to edit *Vanity Fair* and, eight years later, she was appointed editor of the *New Yorker*. In 2008, she co-founded the online news site the *Daily Beast*; there she created Women in the World, a platform for women activists, artists, entrepreneurs, CEOs and dissidents. She resigned from *Beast* in 2013 to concentrate on her roles as CEO of Women in the World and Tina Brown Live Media.

I was a rebel and I was expelled from three boarding schools. That kind of subversiveness is useful – you should always question everything and push boundaries. I regard getting slung out of those schools as a badge of pride because they were such uptight, upscale boarding schools that any budding journalist would want to rebel.

Looking back, I suppose I was fearless – or, more accurately, reckless! I would be invited to events and as an unassuming young woman I could fly under the radar.

Initially, I wanted to be a playwright but I turned to journalism as a way to get paid for writing. When I started out, I wouldn't have described myself as ambitious. Looking back, I suppose I was fearless – or, more accurately, reckless! I would be invited to events and as an unassuming young woman I could fly under the radar. No one was expecting me to write a sharp piece or something insightful – it was fun surprising them.

The meetings I had to go to when I was young were often full of pale, stale males hogging the conversation. I always knew I had good ideas, but at the beginning I feared to voice them. With each year, I held back less and less. Early success does create a bit of pressure, but I get a lot of energy from my work and I also do what I love. Regardless of my career, I would be digging into news sites and devouring anything and everything on my Twitter feed. I certainly didn't think of myself as a trailblazer. I just knew what I wanted and went for it with everything I had. Early on with *Vanity Fair*, when I was constantly being asked 'When is your magazine going down the toilet?' we had a big photo story about to go to press on the love marriage of Nancy and Ronald Reagan – wonderful pictures – when word came that the White House was thinking of withdrawing permission. I took the chance of flying to DC the next morning, hugging the dummies, and the Reagans, bless 'em, relented.

I have been lucky to work with many great writers. I've learned to trust my instincts when it comes to hiring talent. A good writer has a distinctive voice and a point of view that leaps from the page. I want to read a piece and be challenged to think about something in a new and different way. Dominick Dunne did it for me, and his piece on the murder of his daughter was one of those breaks that lifted *Vanity Fair*.

The thing I feel proudest of is my work at the *New Yorker*, finding the old guard so in touch and introducing incredible new talent. Now Women in the World is my passion project. It builds on everything I've done before. It's a live publishing experience – and giving incredible women a platform to share their stories has been one of the most rewarding things I've done.

Journalism remains a great career. We need more long-form journalists in the digital age, people who are thinking critically and synthesising information, not just spitting out clips for the 24-hour news cycle. There are also new and exciting platforms, such as VICE (where my daughter works) and Medium, which are finding different ways to cover stories or find voices.

Yes, I do push people, but I've found many who didn't realise how very good they are until they're asked to go that extra mile.

It's important to lead by example. If I'm not willing to stay up all night to make something perfect, why would anyone who works for me do that? Yes, I do push people, but I've found many who didn't realise how very good they are until they're asked to go that extra mile – make that two miles, and raining! The extra effort is that bit that can be magic and make the product a cut above the rest.

That's why I'm not afraid to take chances and to push staff – and magazine audiences – outside of their comfort zones. I was often put in charge of magazines when their influence was waning. My job was to reinvigorate and revive those brands. Some might see the choices I made as 'brave', but they were choices that I thought were imperative to bring magazines such as *Vanity Fair* and the *New Yorker* into their next era. I think women take more flak – you're bitchy, you're bossy, you're 'Stalin in high heels', as I was called (accurately!). I don't have a Google alert.

I have been much moved by the women I've met through Women in the World – women like the mother whose daughter went on jihad in Syria, and the Israeli and Palestinian mothers who lost their sons and work together for peace. We've been graced by the support of Meryl Streep – who's been with us from day one, as has Hillary Clinton – and more recently Helen Mirren, Angelina Jolie, Cate Blanchett, Christine Lagarde and Condi Rice.

You can't hear from those women without being driven to do better and more with your life. With Women in the World, I am trying to give a platform to women on the frontlines of international news to tell their own stories, and help them reach a larger audience to effect change. In 2015, we brought our summits to London and New Delhi.

My husband, Sir Harry Evans, is the greatest editor I know and our partnership and his belief in me has allowed me to be successful both personally and professionally. He wants me to slow down. I say I might when he does, but I continue to have new ideas and to find projects that make me feel alive. Besides going global with Women in the World, I'm in the middle of writing my memoir, *Media Beast*, and I know I have a few more books in me.

Tina's Object

A slim black *Economist* diary. I've been re-ordering it since 1980 and it's very personal because when I first met my husband, one of the things I fell in love with was the little black *Economist* diary in which he would write all his appointments, including when he was seeing me, and our little anniversaries. Even now that I have calendars online, I don't feel fully grounded without my little, lateral view *Economist* diary. At weekends I take my digital calendar and fill up my *Economist* diary for the week. I have my initials in gold on the front and my husband has his, with his initials on the front, so we don't get them mixed up. I like the fact that it's British. The anniversaries inside are British anniversaries and the tube map is at the back. I sometimes find myself in meetings looking at it and it gives me a heartwarming feeling, a sense of being close to my old home.

FRANCHESCA RAMSEY

Writer, actor and YouTube star

FRANCHESCA RAMSEY

Franchesca Ramsey is a writer, actor and video blogger, based in New York. She has two YouTube channels – Chesalocs, which is dedicated to natural haircare, beauty and styling (she has long dreadlocks); and another on which she comments on social issues, including race, gender and sexual health, through sketches and pieces to camera. Between them, her channels have more than 250,000 subscribers; in total, her videos have had more than 26 million views. Franchesca Ramsey shot to fame in January 2012 when her video *Shit White Girls Say to Black Girls* went viral. The four and a half minute film was a comic riff on *Shit Girls Say*, the humorous web series created by Canadian writers Kyle Humphrey and Graydon Sheppard. Her version had 1.5 million views in 24 hours and 5 million in five days. It has now been seen more than 11 million times. Franchesca Ramsey, who is known as Chescaleigh to her online fans, continues to make videos about subjects as diverse as cleaning your hair with washing soda, training for half marathons and safe sex, appearing as herself and as a range of characters. She is also a host on MTV's news channel, Decoded.

I grew up online. I learned to code when I was in eighth grade [13–14 years old] and I kept an online journal all through middle and high school. I started my YouTube channel in my senior year at the University of Michigan, where I was studying acting. I was very active in the online dreadlock community – although, oddly, I was one of a minority of black people who were involved – and I thought video was a great way of showing what was working and what wasn't in managing my hair.

After that, I studied graphic design at the Art Institute of Miami and began doing standup. I won a YouTube contest in 2008, the prize for which was to fly to Los Angeles and work the red carpet at the Emmys. It was awesome, and I realised that this was what I wanted to do. In 2011, I was one of 25 winners of YouTube's NextUp Creators Contest, winning money to help fund video production and a four-day training camp, all incredibly useful. I was interested in how you could use comedy to approach subjects such as body image, safe sex and self-confidence.

Shit White Girls Say to Black Girls was an attempt to reflect my experiences as a girl growing up in the suburbs; I actually grew up in West Palm Beach. The video reflected all the small insults and micro-aggressions that black women are subject to. It was very personal. I certainly didn't expect it to be such a hit. For a start, *Shit Girls Say* had already been out for several months and I thought that meme was over. I didn't realise how many other girls had had those experiences. That was one reason for its success. The other was that white women told me that it was a kind of lightbulb – 'Oh, wow! This is how I sound!'

I was interested in how you could use comedy to approach subjects such as body image, safe sex and self-confidence.

Tons of people were offended by it but I think comedy is a great way to make things that are difficult to talk about a little more digestible. Some people did misunderstand me. They think I hate white people. I don't hate anyone. They project their own issues on to me, which can be difficult, but I hold on to what my mom said to me: 'Don't worry when they talk about you; worry when they don't talk about you.'

The success of *Shit White Girls Say* meant that I got an agent, a manager, television gigs and speaking engagements, and I could quit my full-time job. YouTube is a fantastic, democratic medium. Anyone can pick up a phone and start making a video. People who wouldn't get a look-in with traditional media can post their creative efforts and see if they can start acquiring an audience. It's much more collaborative than old media. You're not talking at your audience; you're talking to them. On Decoded I tend to pose a question and then respond directly to comments. My audience informs the work I do – so I'm fortunate that they're smart and thoughtful! Around 70 per cent are female and most are in high school or college, but I have older and younger followers. A lot of my followers are young black women.

People who wouldn't get a look-in with traditional media can post their creative efforts and see if they can start acquiring an audience. It's much more collaborative than old media. You're not talking at your audience; you're talking to them.

I wouldn't recommend anyone to become a vlogger to get rich and famous. I was producing videos online for six years before *Shit White Girls Say*. You need to love doing it, and you also need to be able to say something original, in a way that's innovative, smart, funny and lets the audience participate. When I'm on Decoded, viewers send gifs or video responses or Snapchat comments. I have long conversations on Twitter with people I have never actually met, yet I feel I know them.

A lot of my audience are people who have been with me a long time. They say things like, 'I remember before you and Patrick got married…' They know quite a lot about me but I am definitely more private than a lot of vloggers. I don't disclose where I live in New York. When I had a job, I didn't say what I did. I am quite careful about what I reveal. I do always think about whether it's OK for my parents or my employer to see my videos. My parents watch

them and my mom is my biggest cheerleader. She always urged me to work really hard, to be professional and poised. I talk to her every single day.

I think it's really important – especially if you're putting yourself out there – not to compare yourself to anyone else. You can't measure your success by what someone else is doing. The best tip I know for success is to surround yourself with people who are creative and hard-working. It's quite isolating being a video blogger, so it's important to collaborate whenever you can.

Of course feedback isn't always kind and, online, there can be a lot of unpleasantness, especially when those responding are anonymous. I do sometimes check out when people are saying nasty things, when they clearly just want to fight with you. There are some battles that are not worth fighting, some people with whom it's simply not worth engaging. There are a lot of sad strange folk on the internet, who devote way too much time to people they're supposed to hate. But I manage to take a positive attitude – clearly, I'm doing something that keeps them coming back.

Franchesca's Object
My dog, Kaya. She's half Yorkie and half Dachshund and she motivates me. She weighs about 3kg [7lb] and she's ferocious. She sets her own terms for everything and she's not afraid of much bigger or more impressive-looking dogs. She's very attentive, always listening. She barks immediately if a package is delivered or if she hears something on the street. She's intuitive and smart and spunky and that's how I aim to be – aware of what's going on and not afraid to speak up.

TARYN DAVIS

Charity leader and founder,
American Widow Project

TARYN DAVIS

Taryn Davis is the founder and executive director of the American Widow Project, which supports the widows and widowers of American service personnel. She grew up in San Marcos, Texas, and married her high-school sweetheart, Michael, shortly after he joined the US Army. In May 2007, when she was 21, he was killed in a roadside bomb attack in Iraq. Today, the American Widow Project supports 1,600 service widows and widowers across the US with events, befriending and educational programmes. Taryn's work has been widely celebrated in the media and she has received multiple awards as a leading social innovator.

I was an awkward, introverted child and as a teen I had a fear of not being accepted or liked, because of not wearing the right sort of make-up or something like that. I was not the sort of person you'd think would start an organisation. But the one good thing about grief and loss is that you just don't care what people think any more. You have no fear.

I had seen Michael a month before he died, when he was home on leave, and I was instant messaging him an hour and a half before he was killed. He broke off, said he had to go, which I knew meant he was being sent out, but that was his job so I thought nothing of it. I went over to my parents' house for dinner, which I often did because I was still at college. And then at ten o'clock, the call came. It was a neighbour to say I had to get home because some people were there who needed to speak to me.

There were two of them, men wearing the uniform Michael had worn to marry me 18 months before. They told me he was dead. All I could think of was talking to Michael about this man who couldn't compose himself to tell someone that her husband had died. They asked me to sign some paperwork and then they gave me a folder called 'The Days Ahead', which had photos in it of coffins and urns.

I didn't eat or leave the house. I pushed away my family. I didn't want to go through losing anyone again.

After the funeral, I thought I was going to die. I didn't eat or leave the house. I pushed away my family. I didn't want to go through losing anyone again. I was just sitting on the couch in front of movie channels. Physically, I'd given up. And then one day I googled 'widow' to see what other people thought it meant. It said: 'Did you mean 'window'?' I tried images – they were mostly of spiders. I felt like I was the only young widow in the world.

The average age of US service men and women who have been killed in combat is 26, and 51 per cent of all service personnel are married. About 3,000 people had died in Iraq and Afghanistan at that point, so I figured that there must be at least 1,000 other young widows out there. After a few months, I went to see the only other one I knew, whose husband had been in the convoy with Michael. We'd been stationed in Alaska together when they were training. I found her sitting holding her 11-month-old baby. We cried a lot and I recognised something in her. She looked dead behind the eyes, like I did.

We started talking about our memories and I saw something then, a spark. I wanted to find out what could make that come back. I had a 'death gratuity' of $100,000 from the government and I used that to start the American Widow Project, tracking down other young service widows and asking a friend to help me make a documentary. I filed for tax exemption to start a non-profit and set up a website. In the summer of 2008 we held our first event. Thirty people came, most of us in our early 20s.

We did zipwiring and shooting rapids and watching bats come out at sunset. We needed to be forced into situations that would make us live. At the end of the weekend we watched the

152

documentary. People who'd met as strangers were hugging and crying and laughing. I knew then that none of us would feel any more that we were the only young widow.

Since then, the AWP has run about 70 four-day events, all free of charge. We keep them small and intimate so the places get booked in minutes but it's what happens in between that's most important. Many friendships have developed and we've started programmes to help people go back to college. We went off to build homes after Hurricane Katrina. Some members have remarried and other widows have been their bridesmaids. Members have started businesses and AWP friends have been their first customers.

> *So many widows live with the fear that if they decide to live again, other people might think they've forgotten their husbands. We reassure them that we know they haven't, however they decide to spend their lives.*

So many widows live with the fear that if they decide to live again, other people might think they've forgotten their husbands. We reassure them that we know they haven't, however they decide to spend their lives. In keeping your husband's legacy alive, it's easy to overlook your own life. We don't give ourselves any option but to live. We're not letting what has happened to us determine everything about us in the future. We're defining for ourselves what it means to be a young widow.

I never wanted AWP to grow into some enormous organisation – you don't want there to be more widows. At the height of the Iraq and Afghanistan conflicts there were between 30 and 40 deaths a month. Now we're seeing 22 suicides a day among those who have left and are still in the military. There are more non-combat than combat widows now. We've also had Gulf War and Vietnam widows asking to join. I created AWP hoping that one other widow

would have it easier than I did. Now I look back and I think, 'How the hell did I do that?'

Taryn's Object

The tattoo on my back of Michael's wedding ring, with words from a Ralph Waldo Emerson poem. I don't have Michael's wedding ring. The army tells personnel not to wear them on combat missions, because they can catch the light or snag on equipment. When I got Michael's effects – they sent back what he was wearing – I told them that if he had been wearing his ring, they should leave it on his body. I had a feeling he wouldn't have taken it off. That turned out to be right, so he was cremated with it and then I threw it with his ashes in the river.

At his funeral, I read a quotation from Ralph Waldo Emerson's poem 'Threnody':

The eager fate which carried thee
Took the largest part of me.
For this losing is true dying.

The tattoo on my back runs from my shoulder blade to the middle of my spine and has that quotation running round the wedding band. Neither of us had tattoos and I came from the sort of family where you get a tattoo and your parents disown you. But I had it done two months after his death. I felt it was an object that nobody could take away from me. It was a sign of what I had gone through and it's something that will never leave me, a sense that he's always there.

I had it done all in black and white. The only thing in colour is the wedding band. It has faded with time. The better I've gotten in life, the more it's faded. But it's still there.

DR MAGGIE ADERIN-POCOCK

Space scientist

DR MAGGIE ADERIN-POCOCK

Maggie Aderin-Pocock is a space scientist. Since February 2014, she has presented the long-running television programme on astronomy, *The Sky at Night*. Born in Britain to Nigerian parents, Aderin-Pocock attended 13 different schools before going on to study physics at Imperial College London and taking a PhD in mechanical engineering. She has worked in private industry, on government contracts and in academic research. While she was lead scientist at Astrium, the optical instrumentation group, researching for the European Space Agency and NASA, she started giving talks to children and young people, which led to her becoming a television presenter. Since having her daughter in 2010, she has concentrated on consultancy and on her career as a presenter and a promoter of science.

I always wanted to be an astronaut. I still do. It's been the driving force in my life. I applied to go to the International Space Station when Tim Peake was chosen – but he's a lot thinner than I am. I knew I was interested in science really quite early in my life, and that space was my main focus. I thought *The Clangers* [the children's television animation featuring puppets that spoke in whistles and lived on a moon-like planet] was fantastic.

Our sun is one of 200 billion stars in our galaxy. What else is out there? What are the possibilities?

The moon and I have a personal relationship. I am mesmerised by it. Not long after I was born, people landed on the moon and I grew up with a sense of the possibilities of space. I felt strongly that it was this amazing thing waiting to be explored. I lived mostly in London and you don't see much of the night sky there, but you can usually see the moon. When I was studying for my GCSEs, I found a local telescope-making class and I used to go every week – ten middle-aged men and me, polishing and grinding our mirrors. Later, I spent a wonderful six months working in Chile on one of the huge telescopes in the desert, and I used to watch the moon rise over the mountains. Often, the moon was my only companion.

My father came to Britain from Nigeria, hoping to study medicine, but it didn't happen. He took a job in a restaurant, became a manager and then started his own business. I was lucky that he was ambitious for me. When I was three, he used to ask me which university I wanted to go to. But I was dyslexic at school and I was put in a remedial class. My parents split up when I was four and after that, I changed schools a lot – but that was quite useful because I was able to give myself a promotion. I'd been in the lower streams but when my new school asked what class I should be in, I said the top stream.

Science saved me. I had a problem with reading and writing and once you have a label or a stigma, it's hard to shake it off. At the age of about ten, I put my hand up in a science class when we were asked a question about the weight of a cubic centimetre of water. I thought it was easy, but no one else had their hands up so I put mine down again. But then I thought, 'No, I know this.' Then, 'If I can do this, what else can I do?'

At school I used to say I wasn't English, I was Nigerian, even though I'd never been to Nigeria and couldn't speak the language. I wanted to make the point that I was proud of being different. There were no other black children in the class and I was teased. Looking back, that may have been part of the attraction of space. You don't see the barriers. I loved *Star Wars* partly because it involved all kinds of different people working together.

Physics truly is the study of everything, from the smallest particles to the expanding universe. There is demand for physicists in all walks of life – it would be useful to have more physicists in parliament, for example, because politicians have to make scientific decisions. I began a presentation at a conference recently by saying, 'I know nothing about art, literature or history,' which is a shocking thing to say, yet people say that sort of thing about science all the time and don't think there's anything wrong with it.

The moon and I have a personal relationship. I am mesmerised by it. Not long after I was born, people landed on the moon and I grew up with a sense of the possibilities of space.

Every culture has been fascinated by the magic of the night sky, interpreting its beauty and mystery in many different ways, but pretty much everywhere there has been this sense of 'wow!' – and the more we learn, the more 'wow' it is. Our sun is one of 200 billion stars in our galaxy. What else is out there? What are the possibilities? We are so much closer now to making that discovery.

I have been lucky enough to work on the James Webb telescope, Hubble's big brother, which I think will transform our knowledge of the universe once it launches in 2018. Around 5,000 scientists have worked on this project across the world. I collaborated with people in Germany, France and America. I do hope our little piece of it works because it will be fired a million miles away from earth so if anything goes wrong, we won't be able to fix it.

More than 2,000 exoplanets [those that orbit stars other than our sun] have been identified so far, of which a few thousand are the right size to support life and are orbiting in the habitable zone. Some people are scared by the idea that there could be life out there and some people are really excited. I'm one of those who are excited.

When I was pregnant, I was effectively doing three jobs and I decided something had to give, so I stopped doing research in industry. I miss engineering – there is a pure joy in building things in the lab – but I love presenting *The Sky at Night*, which is not only the longest-running television programme but has had the longest-running presenter. In 57 years, Patrick Moore missed just one episode. It has many die-hard fans and we explain the universe in a very friendly way. My daughter travels everywhere with me. Before she started school she had done 120 flights, including to Tokyo and Hong Kong, and to the States many times. I give lots of talks and speak to tens of thousands of young people a year. And I'm devising a TV cartoon, inspired by *The Clangers*, with the working title *Interstellar Ella*, about a girl who travels the universe on her space scooter. I am hoping to explain cosmology to four to seven-year-olds.

Maggie's Object

My wedding dress. I married my husband 12 years ago, after we met doing our PhDs in mechanical engineering. I wanted to wear something simple, a concept of my own. I can't sew for toffee and getting something made to measure in the UK was way beyond my budget. Then I thought about stopping off on one of my many trips and getting it custom-made in Thailand to my own spec, and that sums up quite a lot for me – take your dreams to the stars, be an opportunist, see how far you can get.

CLARISSA WARD

CNN senior international correspondent

CLARISSA WARD

Clarissa Ward is an award-winning television foreign correspondent. Born in London, she spent her childhood there and in New York, attending boarding school in the UK and then Yale University. She began her career at Fox News, subsequently moving to ABC and CBS before joining CNN as senior international correspondent based in London. She has reported many times from Syria, dodging gunfire and bombs and, on one occasion, confronting a jihadist with evidence that he had killed prisoners he claimed to have been protecting. She has also covered events in Yemen, Iraq and Afghanistan; the revolution in Ukraine; the Russian incursion into Georgia; and the 2011 earthquake and tsunami in Japan. She has lived and worked in the Middle East, Russia and China and speaks six languages, including Arabic, Russian and Mandarin.

For most of my childhood I wanted to be an actress. I loved plays and film and I was a member of the National Youth Theatre. But then I was in New York when 9/11 happened and that was it. From then on there was never any doubt about what I wanted to do. I had always been interested in different cultures but from that moment I wanted to try to facilitate better communication. Reporting became a vocation.

I started at the very bottom – subterranean. I was a freelancer on the overnight desk at Fox News. I would go in to work at midnight and come out at 9am and then go to my Arabic lessons. My body didn't take well to the overnights. I hadn't dreamed of working at Fox but I didn't want to wait. So I did that for a year and then, to their credit, Fox sent me to Iraq to produce and I got the opportunity to go on air. I was working during Thanksgiving, Christmas and New Year and that happened to be the time that Saddam Hussein was executed.

I would go in to work at midnight and come out at 9am and then go to my Arabic lessons.

I have a natural aptitude for languages. My grandmother was a linguist and a pianist. I was useless at the piano but I have inherited the language ability. Growing up in New York and London also gave me an ear for mimicry – I can

sound more American or English, depending where I am. I speak different languages with varying degrees of fluency – French and Italian very well; I have a good understanding of Spanish; Russian and Arabic conversationally. Mandarin is the toughest. I lived in China for two and a half years and fought hard to get the basics but you lose it if you're not there. I know that my reporting has added depth when I speak the language of the people I'm working with. A language can also teach you a lot about a culture.

It's a man's world and I kind of like that, being one of the guys. I tend to eschew sexuality.

Sometimes being a woman is a drawback. Occasionally, it's clear you're not going to get the interview and then you just have to suck it up. But quite often it makes things easier. Wear an abaya in Syria or Sinai and when you go through checkpoints, you can pretend to be asleep in the back of the car. Sometimes, being a woman gives you access to 50 per cent of the population that your male colleagues might not be able to approach. The women may not want to go on camera, but they know who's who, who's responsible. I remember being in a house on the outskirts of Aleppo when the shelling was getting closer. The men became tense and they were smoking heavily and arguing with each other. To get away from the bickering and simmering violence, I went to sit with the women. They were petrified. One was rocking back and forth, hugging a pillow and crying. Others were rubbing each other's shoulders or trying to keep themselves distracted. I felt their fear and claustrophobia and it gave me a quite different perspective.

I am frightened a lot. I hate shelling and bombing. I don't like being on the front line. It happens that I end up there because that's where the stories are. I've lost a lot of friends and it takes its toll. In the moment, fear can be useful because it helps you to get out of trouble but it can also paralyse you. I try to be rational — to think that it would be very unlucky if the bomb dropped on the very building where I am — and, of course, while you have to take risks, you also calculate them. When I confronted the jihadist about the men he'd killed, we'd worked out how much time it would take us to get back to the border. It is very difficult to look in a man's face and call him a liar, but it was important to do it — not least because that was when it became clear that the war in Syria had reached a turning point, the people's uprising had been completely hijacked and we were entering a new phase.

> *I am frightened a lot. I hate shelling and bombing. I don't like being on the front line. It happens that I end up there because that's where the stories are.*

I am very conservative about the way I dress and behave in the field. It's a man's world and I kind of like that, being one of the guys. I tend to eschew sexuality. Some women reporters have made it their trademark — there is a fashion in the US for breathless war correspondents with plunging cleavages. I resent it, because it creates a bad impression on people overseas whose stories we're covering. And it creates the wrong idea about what is needed for success. A producer once asked me why I always wear my hair up. The answer is that I have more important things to think about. Some day maybe we'll go out for dinner with friends and I'll wear my hair down, but right now I'm at work.

It really troubles me when I hear educated people in the US or the UK saying things about Muslims that are rooted in fear. I worry about how the media is contributing to that. I wish people could experience all the wonderful interactions that I have had — and that is what drives me, really. I want to tell the geopolitical story, but I also want to make our viewers understand their fellow human beings. Fundamentally, I think people are open to understanding others and seeing things from their point of view. It's all about exposure. We need to open up to others.

Clarissa's Object
A little paper with sura yasin [one of the chapters of the Qur'an] written on it, given to me by a very sweet Syrian woman who believed that reading it over and over again protects you. During the phase of the civil war when it was still possible to get into Syria, I was being hidden in a safe house, waiting to be smuggled out. Trying to cross a border illegally in the middle of the night is not fun. I have always held on to the sura. My understanding of written Arabic is not very good but this woman's gesture is more important than what the sura actually says. She gave the paper to me in a spirit of love and out of a desire to protect me, a stranger, someone she didn't know but wanted to help.

TRACY EDWARDS

Round the World sailor

TRACY EDWARDS

Tracy Edwards skippered the first all-women crew to compete in the Whitbread Round the World Yacht Race in 1989. Her boat *Maiden* won two legs of the race and came second overall; she became the first woman to receive the Yachtsman of the Year Trophy. Tracy Edwards learned to sail as a stewardess on a charter yacht after being expelled from school, and was the first woman to race around the world on a Maxi (a boat of at least 21 metres). Her Whitbread triumph with *Maiden*'s 12-woman crew broke a number of records. A subsequent attempt to win the Jules Verne trophy with an all-female crew in 1998 foundered when their mast broke near Cape Horn. In 2014, she discovered that *Maiden* was decaying in the Indian Ocean and launched a successful public bid to restore the yacht and return it to Britain to be used to raise funds for girls' education.

My father died when I was ten and my world collapsed. My mother married a man I loathed and we moved from Berkshire to a village in Wales. My stepfather was an alcoholic, violent and abusive. I didn't do the sensible thing and tell my mother. She was working as a cleaner, in a shoe shop and behind the bar in a pub and he would come in and drink away what she earned. I was bullied at school, so I was being beaten up at home and beaten up at school. I became very rebellious, aggressive and angry. After I was expelled, my courageous mum launched me off backpacking.

I ended up working in a bar in Piraeus. I'd see all these beautiful yachts in the harbour but I didn't think they were anything to do with me because I thought I was worthless and didn't deserve any luck. But then someone who used to come into the bar offered me a job. His girlfriend was the cook and, although I was 17 and had no experience, she gave me the job. Within days, I thought, 'This is what I want to do for the rest of my life.' I don't think it was immediately the ocean or the boat – it was the people. I'd always felt I was on the outside looking in. After my father died I never seemed to fit in. I wasn't very good at anything. On the boat there were people from diverse backgrounds who'd all fallen into sailing; no one had planned it. I didn't feel judged.

There are a lot of women in the charter world, because it's a skivvy's job. But then I moved into racing – for fun, initially, until a boyfriend pointed me towards a boat that had done the Whitbread. He suggested I speak to the skipper and in 1985–6, I took part in the Whitbread as a cook. My first reaction was, 'Why don't more women do this?' – not from a feminist point of view, initially, but just because it's such fun. Through a mutual friend, I met Howard Gibbons, who had fingers in a lot of pies. He was quiet and balanced and thoughtful where I'm very emotional, yet we formed this bizarre partnership. If Howard saw I was going to lose my temper, he made sure it happened out of sight of any journalists. He helped me harness my anger and turn it into something really good.

> *My first reaction was, 'Why don't more women do this?' – not from a feminist point of view, initially, but just because it's such fun.*

It was difficult to get sponsorship – people were worried we'd kill ourselves. Even people I liked didn't believe we could do it. Journalists were having bets on whether we'd get to the first stop. *Maiden* wouldn't have got anywhere without King Hussein of Jordan [Royal Jordanian Airlines became the project's sponsor]. He was interested in everything and he was the person who persuaded me to be the skipper. I intended to be the navigator, but a year before the race we were having dinner and I was worrying that I couldn't find a skipper. He said, 'You're deluding yourself and putting off the inevitable. You already are the skipper; you're just faffing around about a title.' So that's how I became the skipper and the navigator – which is unusual because the reason you have a skipper and a navigator is so the skipper can blame the navigator.

On the second leg we were beyond determined, and we came in 36 hours ahead of our nearest rivals. By the halfway point, we led by 19 hours.

We were the only team that stayed together for the whole race. It had been so difficult for us to get to the start line that it bound us together. We were third on the first leg, coming into Uruguay, and everyone was having a party, delighted that we'd made it – but we were gutted. On the second leg we were beyond determined, and we came in 36 hours ahead of our nearest rivals. By the halfway point, we led by 19 hours. And then I made a couple of bad navigational mistakes and we finished in second place overall. It was still the best result for a British boat since 1977 and, sadly, it remains the best result for an all-female crew.

It was easier to find sailors this time because Maiden had inspired a whole generation

I withdrew from sailing for some years after that because the pressure was so intense, not least over what to do next, and I wasn't handling it well – but then Howard called me about the Jules Verne Trophy [for the fastest circumnavigation of the world in any type of yacht] and we started putting together the first all-female crew to sail a Maxi multihull. It was easier to find sailors this time because Maiden had inspired a whole generation of girls. We broke so many records and we were 500 miles ahead, knowing that we had really great weather ahead of us, when we broke our mast in the Southern Ocean.

I became a project manager and got involved in a scheme in Qatar to create a nonstop round-the-world race for multihulls. I borrowed £8 million on the strength of the contracts, but the sponsorship was never paid and that pushed me into bankruptcy. It was the worst experience of my life. You become a child – no bank account, no credit cards; you have to deal in cash. I'd left home at 16 with £50, I'd become a self-made millionaire and, now, at 43, I had £43 in my pocket.

Ten years later, I have worked in internet safety and as a speaker. In 2014, I got an email from a guy asking if I knew Maiden was sitting in the Seychelles, abandoned by her owner, bills unpaid. Nothing on the boat has changed – even our names are still on the lockers. We're bringing the boat back to the UK, where we'll use her to promote girls' rights to education. I will continue to be involved, although probably not on the sailing side. I don't really sail now. For me, it's all or nothing. On a day sail, I get seasick.

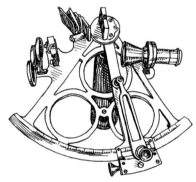

Tracy's Object
A sextant. That's the thing about navigation that I fell in love with. It measures the distance between the sun and the horizon. You hold it up to your eye and measure the angles, then use logarithms. It's like magic. It's sheer joy to guide the boat into harbour, dead centre, having sailed across the Atlantic with just a sextant, seeing what sailors would have seen 200 years ago, totally connected to your surroundings.

PROF NAZNEEN RAHMAN

*Geneticist, doctor and
singer-songwriter*

PROF NAZNEEN RAHMAN

Nazneen Rahman, professor of human genetics, is head of the division of genetics and epidemiology at the Institute of Cancer Research in the UK, and head of the cancer genetics clinical unit at the Royal Marsden NHS Foundation Trust in London. After qualifying in medicine from Oxford University in 1991, she undertook her general medical training in Oxford and London, and she completed a PhD in molecular genetics in 1999. Her research work has been directed towards mapping and identifying human disease genes, with her primary areas of research being breast, ovarian and childhood cancer susceptibility. She is also an accomplished musician. A finalist in the UK Songwriting Contest 2013, she released her album *Can't Clip My Wings* in 2014, gigs regularly and is working on a second album.

Lots of women are drawn to STEM [science, technology, engineering and maths] subjects at school and university, but further up the career ladder, you find fewer women at senior levels. Although that's not confined to science, certain aspects of science have male stereotypes and are thought of as being masculine. It's a very complex, multi-faceted problem – otherwise it would have been solved by now! Quite a lot of unconscious biases continue to exist, and those are the most difficult to overcome – women's perceptions as well as men's.

People are trying to solve the problem by making it easier for women to be like men, but in my opinion, the way forward is to encourage diversity, rather than fit into this constrictive, conservative mode of how things are being done.

Careers in science are organised around pretty traditional male-oriented patterns, which aren't really necessary in this day and age. We can be a lot more flexible. I do a lot of work from my laptop. Conferences could be conducted online, or by video conferencing. But the people at the top – men – don't necessarily have the same need or desire to change the status quo. People are trying to solve the problem by making it easier for women to be like men, but in my opinion, the way forward is to encourage diversity, rather than fit into this constrictive, conservative mode of how things are being done. We need to be proactive, rather than passively hoping that people will change through encouragement.

I come from an academic, traditional family. My father's a doctor, and I decided to be a doctor fairly early on, although I could also have been happy doing other things. I thought I would enjoy it and that was enough for me. I think whatever I had chosen, I'd have made the best of it. Too much choice can be stressful and a lot of people are pressurised into thinking there is one perfect choice.

I've always loved being a doctor, for the combination of problem-solving and the creativity of science, and also being useful. Creative and useful is a perfect mix for me. I can find excitement and some way of being useful in most things that I'm drawn to. I came to genetics by chance. I did my PhD in genetics, really enjoyed it and was fortunate enough to be in an environment that was very exciting. The genes we work on can potentially cause a higher risk of cancer. We can identify this and prevent people from getting cancer in the first place. Working on something that's valued by society has been gratifying.

I don't know anyone of any age who isn't struggling with finding a balance between work and the rest of their lives. It does seem to be something that's of our age. I know I have a sweet spot and once I go beyond it, putting in more hours doesn't make me more productive, while others seem to be able to go on and on. I'd got into a cycle of not working [long hours] but feeling guilty about it, and that seemed to me the worst possible scenario. I started documenting how much time I was spending on what. Via an app on my phone I found out that I was spending a third of my time working. I thought, 'I'm spending enough time on work. That's how much I'm comfortable with,' and that liberated the time I was spending feeling guilty. In terms of balance, I've always been reasonably good at saying no to things. It's a zero-sum game – if you say yes to one thing, you have to say no to others. Every quarter, I sit down and think about how I've used my time, and whether I wish I'd used it better. Thinking about it means I consciously make better use of my time.

Rarely does a day go by when I don't discover a woman who inspires me, right across the generations, from 16 year olds to octogenarians.

Rarely does a day go by when I don't discover a woman who inspires me, right across the generations, from 16 year olds to octogenarians. When I was at school, I found a number of my teachers inspiring – also historical figures, people I read about. I also found music inspiring. The female role models at the time were really dynamic – Annie Lennox, Chrissie Hynde, Kate Bush. The music, the voices, the individuality – you really felt that they were doing what they wanted to do and I think that had more of an influence on me than I realised. Everything seems a little more homogenised and commercialised now – although, having said that, I love Adele.
I've become very interested in leadership, and much more conscious and proactive about how I want to lead. There are lots of different ways to be a good leader, and different circumstances require different types of leadership. One of my mottos is: 'There seems to be almost no way of being a perfect leader and infinite numbers of ways of being an imperfect leader.' I like to lead from the front, and it also feels important to me that there's no part of the work that I wouldn't be happy to do myself, no part that isn't worthy of my time and effort. Being a humane leader is important, understanding that people are inherently inconsistent, and trying to accommodate that. Leading is something one carries on trying to be less bad at on a daily

basis, and one of the roles is being a person that others can complain about!

The thing that has always given me confidence, one of the joys of being a doctor and a scientist, is petitioning for other people, other causes.

Like most people, I can summon confidence in some areas and not others. The thing that has always given me confidence, one of the joys of being a doctor and a scientist, is petitioning for other people, other causes. I think I would have been less effective, certainly when I was younger, in an entrepreneurial role that was simply for myself. When it's for a patient or a scientific truth, I have absolutely no trouble standing up and giving my opinion. When I feel I'm acting for something I really believe in, it makes me strong.

Nazneen's Object
A piano. I would hate to be without one. In recent years I've come to realise how important music is, and what it means to me. There's never a time, whether I'm happy or stressed, that music won't help me in one way or another. Music has been a constant companion in my life. Sometimes it has taken a back seat, when I've been working hard or being a mother – then there has been a resurgence. In the same way that relationships always change, my relationship with music has changed, developed, been very dynamic – but music is an ongoing relationship, a constant companion.

KATHARINE VINER

Editor-in-chief, Guardian

KATHARINE VINER

Katharine Viner is the editor in chief of the *Guardian*, the first woman to be appointed to the job. She grew up in Yorkshire, attended Ripon Grammar School and read English at Oxford, beginning her journalistic career at the age of 21 by winning a competition run by the *Guardian*. She joined *Cosmopolitan* magazine for work experience and stayed on to become features assistant, then news and careers editor, subsequently spending three years at the *Sunday Times* magazine. In 1997, she started on the women's page at the *Guardian*, moving on to edit the Saturday weekend supplement and having a stint as features editor before being promoted to deputy editor in 2008. After running the Saturday *Guardian* for four years, she took off for Australia, overseeing the launch of the paper's online edition there, which became a notable journalistic and commercial success. Some time in New York followed, where she was in charge of the American edition, and then it was back to London to take the top job. Outside journalism, Katharine co-wrote a play with Alan Rickman, *My Name Is Rachel Corrie*, which was based on the emails of a young American activist who was killed in Gaza in 2003. London's Royal Court Theatre put it on in 2005.

I always wanted to do something with words and writing but I didn't know any journalists and I didn't know anything about journalism. I did write my first piece when I was still at school, about the end of O levels [which were being replaced by GCSEs], coincidentally for the *Guardian*, but I didn't join the dots until quite late – no student journalism or anything like that. I won a *Guardian* competition when I was 21 but I entered as a feminist rather than a journalist, because I liked the women's page. The prize was to edit the page for a week, which became two weeks in the end, and that was my lightbulb moment. I loved the immediacy, the pace of the newsroom, and I loved the research, making a story accessible and communicating it. I just found it all so pleasurable.

I was never shy. That helps a lot. It's impossible to say, of course, whether I would have had a different career if I were a man. I think you bring all of your life experiences to everything you do, so being a woman is an important part of that – as is coming from the North, as is living in south London – but whether it's made a difference, for better or worse, I can't tell.

If I could have advised my younger self, I might have said, 'Go into newspapers right away,' although I can't regret being at *Cosmopolitan* and the *Sunday Times* magazine. I'd just moved to London and I met great people and had loads of fun and learned lots of stuff. I didn't see an entry point to newspapers at that time and I did see one in women's magazines. I have never encountered snobbery about that because I'm so obviously interested in serious things.

I might also have said, 'Relax. Don't beat yourself up.' Your 20s often aren't easy because you're still struggling to sort yourself out. Everything got really great when I turned 30.

To get this job, I was chosen by the Scott Trust [the *Guardian*'s owners] and also elected by the staff. I think the staff appreciated that I understand the *Guardian* in my bones. I've lived with it all my life and I care about it deeply and want it to survive. It matters to me and so they know I'll do my best to take care of it. Someone said a funny thing: 'You're the only one of the candidates who seems absolutely to love their job.' It's true. I do love my job. I think people like that exuberance.

In order to set up the operation in Australia I had to think about essentials – 'What is the purpose of the *Guardian*? Who are we in our soul?' – and then articulate that with an Australian accent. We started on a shoestring, with a tiny number of people. I used to write lots of stories under the byline 'Guardian staff', and I was subbing at weekends. Now it's quite a big commercial operation with more than 40 journalists. Then I also had to reimagine the *Guardian* with an American accent. So my pitch for the editorship was: 'What is the *Guardian* now, what is the *Guardian* in essence?'

I think we're about being on the people's side. A tiny élite runs the world, and then there's all the rest of us. I think we have to be on the side of all the rest of us.

> *I think the staff appreciated that I understand the Guardian in my bones. I've lived with it all my life and I care about it deeply and want it to survive.*

Journalism is still a great career for a young person. You get to find out about new things, and learn how to communicate. It's an exciting time. Journalism is flourishing in all sorts of ways. It's more open-access than when I started; you can publish stories online; you can show what your writing's like, what your reporting's like. The business model is challenged but I think the possibilities of journalism are much more open than ever. All free societies need strong news organisations. It's in our collective civic interest that journalism survives, so I think we will work out how to pay for it.

> *I'm working on the way women are treated online and what that means for women on the Guardian, because we have a responsibility. It's a challenge for women in public life.*

Anyone can report something, anyone can write something – and that gives a kind of vibrancy to information. At the same time, people want journalists who are qualified to verify that information and say what really

happened. There's a greater need than ever for good reporting. When there's a major event, all sorts of rumours fly about on social media and you need to know where to go for information you can trust. People are hungrier for information than ever before but also hungrier for someone to tell them what's true and what isn't.

I'm working on the way women are treated online and what that means for women on the *Guardian*, because we have a responsibility. It's a challenge for women in public life. I'm not sure this period of online aggression is going to last for ever. I have a theory that although it may be acceptable now, it won't always be, in the way that domestic violence was once acceptable and isn't any more. It's a completely unreasonable way to expect women to live. If someone came up to a woman in the street, swearing in her face or threatening to rape her, we wouldn't accept it, so we shouldn't accept it online. It's a big issue but I think we'll resolve it.

My only slight regret is that I wish I'd been a foreign correspondent – but I've got an amazing job at the right time in my life, and I've had such fun. I feel like I've grabbed every opportunity. I'm just so pleased!

Katharine's Object
My clackety old grey typewriter, the Grey Fox from Silver Reed, with its own carry case and inky ribbons and plastic elegance. It was a present for Christmas and my birthday combined – my 12th, I think – and I'd stay up late clanging out poems and short stories, and thoughts, essays and ideas, loving words, loving making words my own.

RESHMA SAUJANI

Founder and CEO,
Girls Who Code

RESHMA SAUJANI

Founder and CEO of Girls Who Code, Reshma Saujani was born in Illinois, the daughter of Indian refugees who left Uganda in 1973. After graduating from the University of Illinois, Harvard's Kennedy School of Government and Yale Law School, she worked as an attorney before becoming the first Indian American woman to run for US Congress, in 2010. She went on to become Deputy Public Advocate of New York City and, in 2013, ran a campaign to become Public Advocate on a platform of creating educational and economic opportunities for women and immigrants. When she was unsuccessful, she devoted herself full-time to the national non-profit organisation, Girls Who Code, which she established in 2012 to close the gender gap in STEM (science, technology, engineering and maths) education and empower girls to pursue careers in technology and engineering.

I have always wanted to change the world, and my parents' experience as refugees from Uganda was a factor. They were engineers who came to the United States in the 70s. They didn't have family here and they moved to a small suburb outside Chicago where there weren't a lot of communities of colour. They had to learn the language and how to assimilate and they struggled to find jobs. My mother sold cosmetics, my father was a machinist and I started working when I was 12, as a dog walker.

Young girls need knowledge and mentoring. Often it is better to have a mentor who is just one step above you rather than ten — someone who can help with basic questions.

My father used to read me stories about Dr Martin Luther King, Mahatma Gandhi and Helen Keller and I grew up with admiration for people who live their life in service. I've always been passionate about poverty alleviation and racial equity and, after watching a movie about a powerful female attorney, I decided to be a lawyer. I wanted to go to Yale but was rejected three times. Eventually, I knocked on the door of the dean of Yale and said, 'I have been wanting to come here since I was 12. I work hard. I have great grades. I will make a difference in the world, just give me a shot.' I

had got into a bunch of schools and he said, 'Go to any of them, get in the top 10 per cent and then transfer.' I picked Georgetown in Washington DC because I was passionate about politics and, later, having done my master's at Harvard, I transferred to Yale.

As the daughter of immigrants, I didn't know people who went to Ivy League schools and I didn't have any information. Young girls need knowledge and mentoring. Often it is better to have a mentor who is just one step above you rather than ten — someone who can help with basic questions, such as, 'I want to go to college and major in computer science. Where should I go?' or 'I met someone at an event and I want to intern for them. What should my covering letter say and how many times should I bug them?'

I am a hustler. I am unabashed in my passion for Girls Who Code. I will ask anyone to do anything and will not give up until they say yes. I wanted the CEO of Uber, Travis Kalanick, to speak to our girls. I emailed him until I got a response. He met with the girls and we are hoping to build a partnership together.

Coding is like reading and writing. It's the way in which we communicate and for many jobs, you need this skill set. We want to create gender parity in the computer-science field among graduates, and teach as many girls as we can how to programme. We are well on our way — we've taught about 10,000 girls in over 36 states in less than four years. Girls Who Code helped start the conversation about the shortage of women in tech, and now it's become the conversation that many are having, not just in the tech industry, but in government, across the country and the world.

We want to create gender parity in the computer-science field among graduates, and teach as many girls as we can how to programme.

The most important message that I try to impart to girls is about failure and rejection. We live in a society where boys are taught from a young age to play hard and get comfortable with rejection and failure, and girls are not. And so, as we get older, we don't take leaps in our careers, we don't negotiate our raises, we don't start businesses because we're worried that we'll take someone's money and it won't work out. We don't run for office – what if nobody votes for us? We're stifled by our own fear of rejection and failure. I've taught myself to get comfortable with it by visualising the worst-case scenario. When I was 33 I ran for Congress against a Democratic incumbent, a woman who'd been there for 18 years. It was a tough race and I got my butt kicked. But to go through that type of public failure was transformative, because I didn't die – I was still breathing, eating, sleeping, happy and functioning, so it made me stronger.

The most important message that I try to impart to girls is about failure and rejection. We live in a society where boys are taught from a young age to play hard and get comfortable with rejection and failure, and girls are not.

It was Hillary Clinton's concessional speech in 2008 that motivated me to run. I love Hillary, and one of the things that I respect about her is that she gets beat up every day, ten times a day, and fights on because she's passionate about her convictions. When she gave her speech in a hall in DC, there was a huge crowd and everyone was devastated. She said, 'Just because I failed doesn't mean that you shouldn't try, too.' I was a lawyer working in finance in the private sector. I thought, 'I hate my job, I am not making a difference, I'm not achieving the ideals I set out when I was young. I have fiscal health, so I can take a more dramatic step – it's time.'

I think my toughest fight so far has been to have my son. After my third miscarriage, I was broken. The doctors chalked it up to old age but I started researching and my sister, who is a doctor, dug into my medical records and spotted this antibody in my blood. It turned out that I have a condition called APS. I was getting pregnant easily but, when I got to the eight-week mark, my body attacked the foetus. It was empowering to figure it out and take my health into my own hands. I had to give myself a shot in the stomach every night, which was intense, but I had Shaan and I love being a mom.

Reshma's Object
An A5 notebook. For me, journaling is really important both for my personal and professional life. I have kept a diary since I was a little girl. I write in black and I always have an A5 notebook with me. I even keep one by my bed. Writing helps me to think things out. I write when I am in pain or trying to put ideas together, when I want to remember something or when I am stuck and needing to go to the next place. After I lost my congressional race I was broke, I was humiliated, I was thinking, 'What do I do with my life?' I started writing as therapy and that journal was the basis of my book, *Women Who Don't Wait in Line*.

KAT KAELIN

US Army veteran

KAT KAELIN

Kat Kaelin joined the US military as a teenager and was deployed to Iraq before volunteering to join a new initiative that sent women to the front line in Afghanistan between 2011 and 2014. Female Cultural Support Teams (CSTs) operated alongside Ranger strike forces on night raids seeking out insurgents and terrorists. The task of these small groups of women soldiers was to engage with Afghan women, something considered culturally inappropriate for men by the Afghan population, and gather intelligence. At the time, the US military did not allow women to operate in combat roles, but the CSTs, who were attached to different military teams, were working alongside US Army Rangers, were armed and came under fire. In 2013, the then Defense Secretary in the US announced the lifting of the ban on female service members taking combat roles, a policy driven in part by the success of the CST programme. The first female combat soldiers graduated from Army Ranger School in 2015. US Defense Department figures show that 152 US female troops were killed in the Iraq and Afghan wars. Among them were two CST members.

I'm originally from a small town in rural Nevada and I joined the National Guard when I was 17 because it would pay college tuition fees, although in fact I was awarded a track-and-field athletics scholarship eventually. My training in the local unit in Nevada was in transportation. I knew I was going to be deployed and I thought I'd get it over with, so I volunteered to go to Iraq. I left on 4 January 2007, my 19th birthday, and got back in the September. My experience there was really bad. The men called the women's quarters the 'red-light district' and we were given a rape whistle to carry everywhere we went. When I got back I slipped into a deep depression, but I did get myself back on track.

> *The men called the women's quarters the 'red-light district' and we were given a rape whistle to carry everywhere we went.*

I needed to move on in my life, and a friend sent me a flyer about the Cultural Support Team. I was selected to go on the CST course, and the women I encountered there were all very fit, very determined, very hungry. Meeting these incredible women – to this day I'm still friends with many of them – gave me a huge boost of confidence.

The selection process included psychological tests, academic tests, debates, foot marches, runs – lots of different elements. Many of the women were from the military police or military intelligence. I thought, 'I'm a truck driver, I really don't fit,' but the sergeant major said your existing job didn't matter. They were looking for leadership skills and poise. It was nice to hear it wasn't your job they were interested in – it was you. It was drummed into us that the men saw women as a liability, not fit or intelligent enough to serve effectively. But when we started training with the Rangers to get us set up for active deployment, they were great. Our instructor wanted us to go out and do great things.

Our regiment missions were direct action, aiming to kill or capture the enemy. A platoon loads onto a helicopter or into vehicles, but at the other end you have to hump all your gear, sometimes miles, to the mission location. So being able to carry your own weight is extremely important – if you can't do this, it can tear the whole mission down.

The male soldiers would bring the women and children out as they were clearing the compounds. This is at night, I'm wearing the same gear as male soldiers, and I'm five ten, so I look like a man in my soldier's gear – just like the soldiers who have come to their home and taken their men away. I had to show I was a woman, and explain I was there to protect them, and just to ask some questions. I would have to take my helmet off, let them touch my hair and my face, calming everyone down before going through the sensitivities of searching them for weapons – and often the husbands would have given them cellphones or notes to hide.

Whichever job you choose, you have to educate yourself and continue to learn.

I found multiple things that were mission-essential. The Afghan women knew way more than anyone thought, and we were finding terrorists more rapidly from the information the CSTs got from women and children. The children are so sweet, you feel so bad for them. A child, no matter what country they come from, is innocent. A big piece of me was left there with the women and children. Their circumstances are so terrible. A lot of the people are farmers who just want to live their lives.

I wouldn't say I was afraid, exactly, on my first mission. You don't want to fail, of course, but it was more that we were venturing into the unknown. There were no baby steps. They threw us in – 'Here are your night-vision goggles, follow the person in front of you.' My first fire fight, my legs went to jelly, but then your training comes out and you know exactly what to do. After one of my close friends died on a mission, having to go on that next mission was the hardest. It showed you death is real. It happened to one of your sisters. But fear for me is when my child gets sick.

For all of us, working in CST was personal. Going into this mission meant working among people who were competent and intelligent, who treated you as an equal because you did your job and did it well. People say that women don't go into combat but I got off the same helicopter as the men and was shot at by the same guns. We are officially in support roles but we're out there. Our successful group of women has helped to open things up so that now women graduate from Ranger School, and

there are more possibilities in the future.

I have three daughters and I've always thought about what I'd say if they wanted to join the military. I'd tell them to expect the unexpected. Be as fit as possible, because it can put you above the rest and help your reputation. Your peers will know you aren't a weak link. Whichever job you choose, you have to educate yourself and continue to learn. The military will never be a nine-to-five and you have to adjust rapidly. The main thing in any job is to surround yourself with positive, intelligent people, and there are lots of those in the military. I'm excited for future generations now that doors are opening for younger women. The main reason I left the army after ten years was that I didn't think I'd be able to feel as fulfilled again as I was by the CST mission. It was a good ending point.

Kat's Object

My flag and unit patch. On all military uniforms you have the American flag on a patch on your shoulder. As well as your flag patch, you have your unit patch Velcroed onto your shoulder, just underneath the flag, so when you're looking for someone with night-vision goggles, you can find them – of course you can see it in daylight too, but we worked at night. Our call sign was simply the letters CST. The number of women in the military is small, and the number in CST was even smaller, and no one else can wear that patch. Being able to see both my country's flag and my partners' call signs was very important. I'm very proud of my country. Being an American has given me the opportunity to do what I did – to be groundbreaking.

BARONESS GAIL REBUCK DBE

Chair of the publishing group,
Penguin Random House UK

BARONESS GAIL REBUCK DBE

Gail Rebuck is chair of the publishers Penguin Random House UK and sits on their Global Board of Representatives and the Group Management Committee of Bertelsmann Media Group. She was chair and CEO of Random House in 1991–2013 and a non-executive director of BSkyB in 2002–12. Gail is currently a non-executive director of Koovs Plc, Belmond Ltd. and the Guardian Media Group. Gail chairs the Council of the Royal College of Art, the Cheltenham Literature Festival and the Quick Reads charity which she founded, alongside World Book Day, on behalf of the publishing industry. Gail was voted Veuve Clicquot Business Woman of the Year in 2009; was awarded a CBE in 2000 and a DBE in 2009; in May 2015 she received the Women in Publishing Pandora Award for significant and sustained contribution to the publishing industry and in 2016 was awarded the Lifetime Achievement Award by the London Book Fair. She was appointed a Labour Peer to the House of Lords in 2014.

Both my parents left school at 13 and my grandfather, who was a refugee, was illiterate – this wasn't a bookish family. Thanks to my mother, however, visiting the library was the highlight of my week. Books were there as a constant in my head, taking me to imagined places outside of the here and now. When a teacher said something about 'when you go to university' my first thought was, 'What's university?' My parents were quite puzzled – hadn't I had enough of books?

At that time, the only way into work for a woman was as a secretary, so after I graduated I did a six-week secretarial course. My first job was as a production assistant in children's books. I was determined I wanted to be an editor, so I went to the editors in the company and said, 'I'll work at weekends, I'll edit for free, if in return you just tell me what I'm doing wrong.' After nine months I got a job as an editor in a guide-book company. After three years the CEO was headhunted by the Hamlyn group and he asked me to go with him to launch a paperback division. I was determined to get an editorial job and give it 110 per cent – which is what I did – but I took a risk and also had someone who noticed that I could do more and gave me a paperback list to edit. I went on to be a co-founder of Century Publishing in 1982, a new publishing house which was eventually acquired by Random House.

As CEO at Random House I used to meet new joiners and I would be so interested in their paths into publishing – and I was often struck that people would want to become commissioning editors, but were waiting for someone to give them permission. My position was always if you've got an idea, follow it through and submit it. Just because it's not your job doesn't mean you shouldn't suggest it! My early career was always about breaking down barriers – not waiting for someone to offer me something, but, in an entrepreneurial sense, starting things and being prepared to make mistakes and move on. If you have an idea, follow it through. The worst that can happen is someone says no, and you'll at least be noticed. Don't feel stultified by a large organisation that's inevitably quite siloed and strict.

This digital, connected age offers young people an explosion of creativity, a fantastic way to express themselves and their vision. Never have the tools been more available. The digital industry is a great democratiser. Young people have finely honed digital and social media skills and are often much better in this field than seasoned professionals who haven't grown up as digital natives. A number of young women I mentor have risen with electrifying speed in their organisations because they embody the skills that businesses are desperate for.

The older generation had a mind-set that you go into a job, start at the bottom and diligently work your way up. That's not how young people see their lives. They are much more flexible, much more entrepreneurial. They come to the workplace with a set of digital skills that are highly prized. When they marry those skills with the millennial sense of self-worth, confidence and passion, they are valued within corporations. And who better than millennials to understand what millennials want to be and consume and how to market to them?

I think there is a big issue around women owning their leadership power. The act of leadership often comes naturally, but considering yourself a leader does not.

Leader is a tag that's attached to me. I think there is a big issue around women owning their leadership power. The act of leadership often comes naturally, but considering yourself a leader does not. Leadership is quite paradoxical – you need a passion for what you do, strategic insight and the ability to inspire and encourage; but at the same time, over the years that I've led organisations, my leadership style has had to modify itself. In times of transformation, you have to be directional, at other times more subtle and relational. You need to know when to lead from the front, when to be more visible, and when to follow from behind. And you need to know what you can't do. The worst leaders are those who don't hire or promote able, challenging people around them. It's teamwork, ultimately, that drives the organisation – but it's also quite lonely being a leader. You work with and depend on your team, but the buck stops with you.

I talk a lot in schools and my advice is don't give up; follow your instincts; never look back, always look forward; follow your passion and lead a purposeful life. When you find what you want to do, keep focused, and be prepared to fail. And when you do fail, fail fast and move on. Don't agonise.

There's a big difference between my generation and those that followed. We didn't have a chart ahead. All we had were the unfulfilled dreams of our mothers to drive us on. Our mothers growing up in the 40s and 50s never had the chance to be the people they could have become, for various reasons – social mores, economics, lack of education. We had few role models. What lay ahead was uncharted territory. We just got on with it. Young women today worry a lot more than I remember worrying. Today we have piles of press about failure and how hard it is to be a good mother, to be this perfect executive, and all these examples – false in many cases – of 'perfection' and 'having it all'. Women today are understandably the angst generation. I say 'good enough' is excellent as far as I'm concerned. Just do your best. You do have to juggle. It is hard work. But you muddle through – it all works out in the end.

Gail's Object
My first paperback edition of *One Hundred Years of Solitude* by Gabriel García Márquez. I hesitated between two books – this one and my first hardcover copy of T.S. Eliot's poetry – but if I have to pick one, it would be the Márquez. When I read it, I was quite young, and it was quintessentially what a novel should be. Novels transport you out of your own life, open your eyes to a whole world of possibilities. I was drawn into this newly imagined reality where nothing was as it should be.

For T.S. Eliot, I was thinking of how poetry goes straight to the heart, touches your soul and changes you in a very deep way. Looking at both books, now, my annotations evoke an entire emotional journey – that's why physical books are so important.

NIMCO ALI

Activist and co-founder,
Daughters of Eve

Nimco Ali was born in Somalia and grew up in the UK, where she studied at Bristol University and went on to work as a civil servant and an independent training consultant. She is the co-founder, with psychotherapist Leyla Hussein, of Daughters of Eve, a non-profit organisation set up in 2010 to support and protect young women from communities that practise female genital mutilation (FGM). FGM is a set of procedures that involve partial or total removal of external female genitalia, including the clitoris and labia, and sometimes also infibulation – narrowing of the vaginal opening by creating a seal by sewing up the labia. It is carried out before puberty, and often on girls very much younger. FGM, which can prove fatal and often leads to medical complications, has been illegal in the UK since 1985, but was formerly considered a mainly cultural issue. Nimco Ali and Daughters of Eve have successfully campaigned for it to be recognised as child abuse.

I had FGM as a seven-year-old, and later saw girls who could have been my younger sisters going through it. I listened to people talking about it, and realised they just didn't get what was needed, but I didn't join in the conversation. Then I started to see my silence as complicity.

It was around early 2011 when I first said, 'I'm Nimco and I'm an FGM survivor.' A lot of people were shocked.

Around 2010, I moved to London and came across a lot of people working around FGM, but there was no strategic planning and I couldn't see what they were trying to achieve. I wanted to educate people, yes, but this isn't a question of ignorance – it's organised crime. I got together with Leyla Hussein, who was working on FGM with the community and young people, and suggested, 'Let's frame the work you're doing around policy.' So we started to do more around working with MPs and policymakers.

It was around early 2011 when I first said, 'I'm Nimco and I'm an FGM survivor.' A lot of people were shocked. Their reaction was, 'But you're so together!' and I said, 'This is what an FGM survivor looks like.' I didn't want to be treated with a lot of sympathetic 'poor you' comments. I wanted to talk about survivors, not victims, and I wanted to prevent it, not just talk about it. This was about protecting girls who were so very, very much ignored. I remembered conversations I was hearing at 11, 12 years old – now I was an adult I could do something about it. I was coming from a UK perspective and once I started using language such as child abuse, a lot of stuff I got back was very hostile. A lot of survivors were horrible to me at the start. I can understand them; it's a very personal thing. Many of them are supportive now.

I want to place the responsibility firmly in the hands of those in the state or public sector who have a duty of care. I had seen community work being done for years, and I knew it didn't work. I remember meetings where the question 'How can we deal with this?' was asked, but the conversations were with men from the community who benefited from FGM in terms of having the power, or with women who were themselves cut, unable to deal with the circumstances, silently complicit, with no way of doing anything about it. It's not up to those communities to police themselves. We had legislation, but no one was using it. People were saying, 'How can mothers allow this? How could people do that?' but I was saying, 'How can you, as a citizen of this country, know a five-year-old is about to be cut and stand by because you're afraid to offend her community? You're telling that child she doesn't matter, you're saying, "That's what happens to girls like you."' And that's more painful than the cut itself. No child should feel nobody cares.

My work was always with the police and with the departments responsible for protecting children. First came redefining FGM with the Home Office as an act of violence; then came defining it as child abuse. It was a way of saying to these girls, 'You're British and we care about you as much as we care about anyone else.' My vagina is British; it doesn't have a different passport! I think that's why a lot of community members were pissy with me. I didn't bother with them. You have to be within the system to understand it. I was saying, 'This is about children. The NSPCC needs to get involved.' I think the NSPCC FGM helpline was the most successful thing we ever achieved. Once the NSPCC (National Society for the Prevention of Cruelty to Children) was involved, we stopped having to keep explaining, over and over again, that this was child abuse.

The first time my picture appeared in a newspaper, I had death threats. I remember thinking, 'They really are going to do this.' I stayed in bed for two and a half days, wondering, 'Is it really worth it?' But I felt guilty and that got me out of bed. I found the strength somewhere to resolve, 'Fuck these people.' If a girl goes through infibulation and something goes wrong and she disappears, we never find out. If something happens to me, at least someone will know.

I think the NSPCC FGM helpline was the most successful thing we ever achieved. Once the NSPCC was involved, we stopped having to keep explaining, over and over again, that this was child abuse.

Some people still blame me but I now think that's their problem, not mine. Having friends I can talk to, people who just listen, has been an immense help, and girls telling me how proud they are is a very humbling experience. A girl came up to me on the Underground, on the Victoria line, and said, 'Are you Nimco, the girl who talks about FGM?' And I thought, 'This is where I get spat on and told I'm a disgrace.' But she wanted to thank me for talking about it. Women who have influenced me include my mentor Efua Dorkenoo. I really respect the work she has done. And I love Caitlin Moran, who is able to talk about things in a way that doesn't freak people out but gets them to understand that FGM is unacceptable, ridiculous, makes no sense. I don't think of myself as a leader but as part of a chain. If it wasn't for all the amazing women who came before me and the women alongside me, I wouldn't be able to do any of these things. I've never used the word leader; humility is the key thing. If you campaign on a personal level, it can become problematic. I'm just playing my role in a bigger conversation, a bigger fight.

Nimco's Object

My grandmother's wedding necklace. My grandmother is the woman I look up to the most and she wore this necklace on the happiest day of her life. It's a sequence of peacocks, attached to each other, made of gold, with green and red jewels. My grandmother lost her mother when she was really young and ended up not going to school as she had to look after her brothers, but none of that stopped her. She's the foundation of how all the women in the family were raised. She's fearless, and believes in equality. I have so much respect for her. I hope one day to have the faith to get married and be in a loving relationship that lasts as long as hers did.

KARLIE KLOSS

Model and entrepreneur

KARLIE KLOSS

Fashion model Karlie Kloss was first approached by talent scouts at the age of 13 in a shopping mall in St Louis, Missouri, where she was brought up. She became famous following her first catwalk appearance for Calvin Klein in 2007, when she was 15. Since then, she has appeared on magazine covers and in advertising campaigns, as well as in numerous fashion shows. Proceeds from sales of the Karlie's Kookies she devised are used to provide meals for children in need all over the world through the FEED Projects charity. Her Kode with Karlie scholarship programme, launched in 2015 in partnership with the Flatiron School in New York, helps teenaged girls learn to code. She also launched the Klossy YouTube channel in 2015, and began a course at New York University.

My family is the reason why I've been able to take this journey, to have this adventure. They've been supporting me and believing in me since long before this career started – and they have been with me for a lot of it. We've travelled the world together. For the first five, six years of my career, when I travelled to shoots and shows, I would always have my family with me – my parents and my three sisters. I would take trips to Paris and have the whole family come. We'd rent an apartment and all stay together. I would come home from work after a long day at fashion week and my mom would be cooking and my sisters would be there.

We still take trips together. The best experiences I've had in my career, I've been able to share with the people I love. We also held family meetings any time I had to make big decisions about my career. It was very important to my family and me that everyone was on the same page. Their constant love and support helped keep me grounded and motivated.

Early on in my career, balancing the life of a high-school student and working model was both overwhelming and exciting. I had a very normal teenage life, even though I was travelling to Europe, Asia, New York very, very regularly. I would go home and have normal family dinner with my parents and my sisters, normal Friday-night sleepovers with my friends, normal cafeteria lunch. I just had very special experiences in addition to that normal life. I just happened to be travelling to Paris on the weekends. It was kind of crazy. I had to turn down a lot of jobs because I needed to be in

school at least half the time. There was never a question of me stopping high school or stopping my studies.

Even after I finished high school, I never stopped learning, even though I wasn't in a traditional school setting. Part of travelling for me is about learning – seeing, tasting, experiencing, meeting people, hearing different languages. There's so much that I learn simply by doing my job. I am a student now – I still work and travel, but I take class in the morning two days a week. My mind is being challenged in new ways. While you can be a student with or without a classroom, I knew I wanted to be back in the classroom with other students to continue exploring big ideas.

Travelling for me is about learning – seeing, tasting, experiencing, meeting people, hearing different languages.

I don't know why I've had this kind of success! There are so many beautiful girls and so many models have come and gone, even during my eight-year career. I still feel like I'm at the beginning, for which I'm very grateful. Building a voice and building a platform is a big part of my motivation, because I want to do meaningful things. I think it's a responsibility that comes with success, and also it's just genuinely who I am, how I was raised. My dad is an emergency-room doctor. He's very smart and has always worked very hard for his family – 12-hour shifts, overnight or all day. That work ethic and that discipline and drive had a huge impact on me. My mum is a very creative artist. She paints and draws and takes photographs – she's very, very special. They raised my sisters and me with good values and good hearts, I think. I've always really valued and respected, in myself and in others, what's on the inside.

Math and science have always fascinated me. I'm very curious about technology and when I started learning about coding, my eyes were opened to how extraordinary it is and how important it is to learn. I quickly realised that understanding code opens doors, especially for women, and there are so few women in STEM – science, technology, engineering, mathematics. I wanted to share what I was passionate about, hopefully excite other girls about coding, and also offer them opportunities to learn. So I made a little video and put it out on my Instagram to say any girls who are interested in coding, send me a video telling me what you would do with this skill set, and we'll pick 20 girls and write scholarships for them to learn how to code. We had hundreds of girls apply and I wish I could have written scholarships for all of them. The hope is that I'll be able to write many, many more scholarships. It's really all about igniting that excitement and passion for learning, specifically in computer science, which I think is often overlooked by girls. I'm biased, but I think girls are better at just about everything! I have three sisters, so I've grown up in a house of girls, and my sisters are brilliant. I think there's nothing we women can't do.

Building a voice and building a platform is a big part of my motivation, because I want to do meaningful things.

I also like learning about businesses – reading the paper and understanding economics and different industries, especially the technology industry. I have yet to start my own big company, but some day I will, I hope. I have a lot of small projects that I'm really passionate

about. Each one starts off as an idea jotted down in my notebook – for me, it's important to get it out of my head and down on the page. As I share these ideas with my team, friends and family, they begin to grow and we ultimately pursue opportunities that allow me to do things I'm passionate about and that create opportunities for others along the way. I hope to have a career in fashion for a long time to come and to be a model for as long as anybody will take my photo! But I also want to do much more learning and working on projects that help other people – as well as enjoying life.

When you're passionate about something, and you're really fulfilled on a personal level too, I think it enables you to be more focused and enjoy every other aspect of your life.

When you're passionate about something, and you're really fulfilled on a personal level too, I think it enables you to be more focused and enjoy every other aspect of your life. Whether you're an artist, a cookie baker, a doctor, a student, or a model, what enables you to be successful, I think, is when you really love what you're doing.

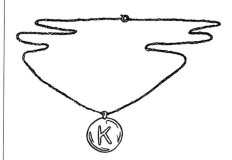

Karlie's Object
My K necklace. My sisters all have K names and we each have one. We all currently live in different places, but whenever I wear my necklace, I feel closer to home.

MINDA DENTLER

Athlete and activist

Born in India, Minda Dentler contracted polio as a child, which paralysed her legs. Her birth mother was unable to look after her and left her in the care of an orphanage. She was adopted by an American family, and surgery enabled her to walk with leg braces and crutches. She gained a management information systems degree from the University of Washington and an MBA in finance and marketing from Baruch College, the City University of New York, and works for a major financial services company. Minda discovered handcycling – cycling powered by the arms rather than the legs – at the age of 28, then progressed to triathlon. She won two USA National Triathlon titles, in 2009 and 2011, and completed her first Ironman Distance Triathlon in 2012. In 2013, at her second attempt, she became the first woman handcyclist to complete the Ironman World Championship in Kona, Hawaii – a feat that involved swimming 2.4 miles, handcycling 112 miles and pushing a racing wheelchair 26.2 miles. Minda now speaks regularly about her experiences, and actively supports the worldwide campaign to eradicate polio.

I have three siblings who are all around the same age as I am. My parents did a great job of trying to make sure that we are all independent individuals – and they didn't give me any breaks growing up. I had the same chore chart as my siblings, and I had to learn to play a musical instrument, as they did. Although I had a disability, no one ever said, 'You can't do that.' They didn't limit me in terms of my goals.

Growing up so different from everyone around me wasn't easy, so I had to focus on things I could control.

My parents have great drive of their own. They adopted two children and had two of their own, and their example gave me some of that drive. But I think it's internal, too. Growing up so different from everyone around me wasn't easy, so I had to focus on things I could control. I focused on being a good student because I knew my ticket to life was education and going to college. I dreamed of living on the East Coast and being part of an international business.

I think having a plan for success is really important. I had a goal of completing the Ironman World Championship in Kona. The first time I went there, in 2012, I failed – and because of that failure, I had to go home, regroup and figure out what I was going to do. I had to change my approach to my training. I found a swimming coach to help me improve my technique, and I found myself some mentors. Triathlon is an individual sport, but as a disabled athlete, I need a lot of support, not just in terms of training but also for things like carrying me in and out of the water. It's not just about your own plan, but also having people to help you – a good team. And on top of that is believing in yourself. In this instance, I was an athlete working towards a goal, but what I did translates into all relationships – work, family. It's about creating systems, then being able to execute them to get to your goal.

There will be times when things are difficult – then it's about mind over matter. Giving up on the Ironman certainly went through my mind, but I have some great friends that inspired me and helped me think about whether it was worth another try. And I didn't want to regret not trying. My mind-set was: 'What can I change, how can I get a better result?'

When I completed the championship, I was ecstatic. I remember having a huge beaming smile on my face. I was in pain, but it didn't matter. I had done it. I thought about all the women who had tried before me, and my own failure the year before. It meant so much to me finally to get it done. In the wider context of my life, it has opened new doors for me. I had the opportunity to meet triathlon champion Chrissie Wellington. She said, 'You have a platform now, you need to use it,' and that really stuck.

I spent the next year figuring out how to share my experience, and change people's views of themselves, and I thought about what issues I could add my voice to. At the time, I was getting connected to the Rotary organisation. I was invited to speak at World Polio Day, and I'm really glad to be part of the effort to eradicate polio. Part of my inspiration comes from my own family. I look at my daughter and I want the best for her. I want the world to be a great place for her. I want her to have the healthiest life possible, and if I can influence other mothers to make decisions that are best for their children, I want to do that. Had I not been adopted, I know I wouldn't be alive. In India, if you have a physical disability, such as polio, your life expectancy is not very high. I have had the surgery I needed, and I now have a responsibility to try to help others.

I look at my daughter and I want the best for her. I want the world to be a great place for her. I want her to have the healthiest life possible, and if I can influence other mothers to make decisions that are best for their children, I want to do that.

When I was first asked to give an account of my experiences at Kona, I felt quite challenged as I'm kind of an introvert. I tried to figure out what I could share – and what I could learn. Even though my story is personal to me, people can relate to the struggle towards a goal that seems out of reach. Using the tools I talk about in my own journey, I think it's possible to achieve any goal, be it a work goal or a personal goal. I get so much energy from the audience when I share

my experience. I can see people processing what I'm saying and know that my words are making a difference. I hope I can inspire others – I really enjoy doing it, and I get something out of it, too. People share their stories with me afterwards, and I'm blown away by that.

As a teenager with a disability, I had a hard time feeling as though I fitted in. If I could go back, this is what I would like to say to that teenaged girl. Never lose your drive and determination, because these will help you overcome any and all challenges that will eventually come your way, especially navigating life as a woman of colour and with a disability. Life isn't easy or perfect. Have faith that setting your goals and working towards achieving them will pay off in the end. Continue to be adventurous and curious, as each experience you have will help you to become more comfortable with yourself. Heed the advice of those you trust, and cherish the friendships that you make in your early adult years, because they will be there for you for life. And don't waste time being negative, or being with negative people. It's just not worth it.

Minda's Object
My handcycle. It represents a turning point for me. I was able to transition from being a sports spectator to being in the game. Learning how to handcycle became a gate to triathlon, which has given me an amazing outlet to achieve something outside my work and my family.

I can push myself and I've been introduced to a whole community of athletes. I'm excited to be a part of it. In sports, I'm not judged by how I look – I'm respected for the effort I put in, and what I achieve. In triathlon I'm competing alongside able-bodied athletes every step of the way. I see sport as an equaliser.

DAME ATHENE DONALD

Professor of experimental physics and
master of Churchill College, Cambridge

DAME ATHENE DONALD

Dame Athene Donald is professor of experimental physics at the University of Cambridge. After grammar school (Camden School for Girls) she studied for her first and second degrees at Girton College, Cambridge. Aside from four years' postdoctoral experience at Cornell in the USA, it is the university where she has worked all her life. Her work has focused on 'soft matter physics', which she has explained as the physics 'of things like cells and food, that a non-scientist would think of as "squishy"'. She was made a professor in 1998, a dame in 2010 and she became master of Churchill College in 2014. Professor Donald is a trustee of the Science Museum, has served as Cambridge University's Gender Equality Champion and is active in promoting diversity in science.

If my younger self could see me now, she would view the life I have had with total incredulity. I was very shy. I didn't expect anything. How could I have imagined I would end up as Master of a Cambridge college? When I was at school, girls weren't expected to have careers. I assumed that after university I'd get a job and then get married. Careers advice was non-existent. I have always just done the next thing. So I try to say to those who are setting out now that it's fine not to know what you want to do with your life.

When I arrived at Cambridge, I consciously worked to stop being so shy. I'd had what would now be called a gap year when I lived away from home and that helped me to practise overcoming my shyness in quite a conscious way and allowed me to appear more confident.

There is still a presumption among many people that childcare is the woman's problem, when it's not — it's the couple's problem.

Marriage gives you what a physicist would call a 'two-body problem' – in other words, two people trying to find a job in the same place. I got married when I was doing my PhD. My husband had a couple of fellowships but I was the one who got the permanent position. He stood back and stopped working for a long time, although it wasn't necessarily what he wanted to do. [They have two children, now grown up.] I have always been uncomfortable being held up as the woman who has done it all – I know what costs were involved.

There is a feeling that science is just a bunch of geeks in a corner, but it's integral to all our lives and the decisions that have to be made.

You do need to marry the right person. I would hope that it isn't the case for all couples that the man needs to give up work – and, of course, it's not really a problem until you have children. But I do think that there is still a presumption among many people that childcare is the woman's problem, when it's not – it's the couple's problem.

There were certainly subtle gender-stereotyping pressures against physics when I was young. In that sense, a single-sex education did help, and I didn't have any brothers to say that physics wasn't for girls. Nowadays, numerous initiatives exist to encourage more girls into science, and people are trying to evaluate them. Bad teaching is a real deterrent, although of course that affects boys and girls. I'm not sure about the importance of role models, not least because I didn't really have any. Talking about the fact that girls are in a minority can help, and focusing on skills, such as being creative. Adjectives are helpful for girls.

But we're all different. The idea of trying to

make physics attractive to women by having advocates wearing short dresses and make-up saying that you can do physics and be feminine would have completely backfired with me. Talking about the issues generally is helpful, pointing out that science is the route to a good job. It's partly just a question of constantly pushing back against the idea that girls do certain things and boys do other things.

> *It's partly just a question of constantly pushing back against the idea that girls do certain things and boys do other things.*

At times, I still feel in the minority. Then finding allies helps. I sat on one very high-level committee chaired by a man who insisted on addressing the group as 'gentlemen' even though two of us were women. I didn't say anything at the time but afterwards I wrote to him pointing out the discourtesy, and I copied in the other woman and the men who'd come up to me afterwards to say how disgraceful it was. The chair replied saying it was just the terminology he was used to and it didn't mean anything. The next time he did it, though, one of the men pulled him up and he never did it again. That was probably more effective than if I'd made a fuss there and then.

I decided to take the job as Master of Churchill because I believe in the Cambridge college system, in the idea of small-group teaching, and I think that it's not for the élite but for the smartest. Churchill is unique in being the only Cambridge college where, by statute, 70 per cent of students read STEM subjects [science, technology, engineering and mathematics]. Each Cambridge college has its own character and, when I visited, I felt I would fit. Some colleges are much more traditional.

Our intake of young women is less than I would like. It's nothing like 50-50 and I would very much like to improve the ratio, but girls don't do physics A level so they can't apply for physics and engineering. We need to work at all levels. We already do an enormous amount of outreach, and we're changing our face a little, I hope – we *look* as if women are welcome, rather than just being a place where women *are* welcome.

I blog and I'm on Twitter because it enables me to reach more people. Some people have referred to the blog as online mentoring. I wrote about non-standard careers, for example, which people said they found helpful. I also try to write in the media about science policy. In science, we're always saying we don't have enough money and it's hugely important to remind the government how much it matters to the future health of the economy. We don't have North Sea oil any more and the banking industry is falling to pieces. Science and engineering is at the heart of our capacity to innovate and grow.

There is a feeling that science is just a bunch of geeks in a corner, but it's integral to all our lives and the decisions that have to be made – whether those are about vaccinations or energy. It's quite important to make sure the information we're getting is accurate.

Athene's Object

A battered collected volume of the novels of Jane Austen. It's a fat tome and it was already pretty well used when I bought it as a teenager at a jumble sale. I have a set of the novels now in smart, single-volume format, but there is something nostalgic and special about this much older, much-loved copy. The novels of Jane Austen are something I turn to, still, in times of stress. There is something about the way she writes that I find soothing. I try to restrict how often I open the pages because there is always the danger that familiarity will breed contempt. But when the science is going badly, colleagues seem to be getting in the way of progress or I'm exhausted from travelling, a little light Austen-reading never goes amiss.

MASHA GESSEN

Journalist, author and activist

MASHA GESSEN

Russian-American journalist, author and activist Masha Gessen is known for her outspoken criticism of Russian president Vladimir Putin, about whom she wrote a book, *The Man Without a Face: The Unlikely Rise of Vladimir Putin*. She is also known for her equally determined championing of human and LGBT rights. Masha grew up in Moscow but her family moved to the US in 1981 when she was 14. She returned to Russia as a reporter in the early 1990s, and is the founder of Russia's Pink Triangle campaign, which encourages supporters of LGBT rights to wear a pink triangle to show their solidarity. Her other books include *Words Will Break Cement: The Passion of Pussy Riot*, which profiles the Russian dissident art-punk group, some of whose members were jailed in 2012 for protesting against the Putin regime. Now back in the US, she writes for the *New York Times*, the *Washington Post*, *Granta* and *Vanity Fair*, among many other publications.

For me to become a writer was sort of inevitable. I'm the fifth or sixth generation of writers in my family; I grew up in the Writers' Union building in Moscow! On the one hand choosing writing as a career seemed very glamorous, but it also seemed pre-ordained. I went to architecture school, but between high school and college, I got a job for a newspaper and I was hooked. I wasn't writing, though. It was only my third year in the US and my English wasn't good enough, so I was doing layout. It was so exciting, seeing the paper come out. I still get a thrill from the physicality of print journalism – having to edit the proofs, taking out a word here, a word there. That's not something you have to do online and it gives you a whole different sense of words. They become objects; they take up space.

Writing gives me a sense – maybe illusory – of acting and it's a huge part of what allows me to keep going.

Our world in general, certainly in a repressive country such as Russia, is constructed in a way that constantly makes you feel helpless. It's a poisonous, horrible way to live. Writing gives me a sense – maybe illusory – of acting and it's a huge part of what allows me to keep going. If I didn't have the outlet of writing and saying what I think, I'd probably be depressed.

I don't think of myself as a particularly courageous person. That's not me being coy. I think it's common in many people who may outwardly seem brave. I've seen it a lot in war correspondents. When I was a war correspondent, I would try to hang back. I never felt an urge to be out there where you might actually get hit, and when I was out there, I tried to get away from those places and talk to people in safer surroundings. I think that's generally a good policy. With my Putin book, I didn't tell anyone I was writing it. My partner, my editor and my research assistant were the only people who knew. Even my best friends and the people I interviewed thought I was writing something about Russian politics in general. That was a reasoned decision. I figured by the time information about the book was available, it would be too late to get rid of me, and they couldn't get rid of the book. Considering I'm walking around, that seems a well-calculated decision.

It's not that I never feel afraid. When Putin first came in, I was harassed really quickly, and it was frightening. The harassment is coordinated and calculated to discombobulate you. The other thing that really frightened me was that my kids were threatened. It's a classic tack and it does work beautifully. I felt a kind of visceral fear and horror I'd never felt before. The risk of my kids being taken away was very small, but I couldn't live with any risk at all, however tiny, so we packed up and moved to the US.

It's been a very odd experience to watch my kids and partner go through the experience of immigration. I know how difficult it is; my parents migrated with me when I was 14 and it was very hard. And I see how fast the process is now. We're two years out of Russia and the two older kids are New York teenagers. Something did happen to them, though. Immigration is a loss of innocence. It becomes a part of you that confirms nothing is to be taken for granted. The landscape of our lives was gone overnight and nothing will ever be quite as permanent again.

Immigration is a loss of innocence. It becomes a part of you that confirms nothing is to be taken for granted.

I want regime change in Russia. It will happen, although I don't think my contribution to it will be considerable. Many people are working towards the same end, and eventually the regime will implode but it's not going to be taken down by us. A smaller goal is to get safe havens and refugee status for LGBT people around the world. There's a worldwide cultural war going on and the refugees from that world are LGBT people. The only places reliably granting them refugee status are the US and South Africa – which is a lifeline for people fleeing African regimes. It's difficult to come to the US from Russia if you are LGBT, and until your refugee status is confirmed, you have no rights, no public assistance. It's a brutal system. A lot of European countries have better systems but don't offer asylum to LGBT people. If they did, the physical proximity of Europe to Russia would make the difference between death and life, safety and security for a lot of people.
Of the things I regret, it's times when I've tried to be cautious and relied on what seemed to be grown-up decisions – not taking a job, not taking an opportunity. So long as you look after your physical safety, which is really important, no opportunity should seem unreasonable. Take anything that seems exciting! Don't play it safe. Things are less predictable than we like

to think. In the 1990s, I was living in Moscow, freelancing for some really good American magazines, but I felt that if I was going to be a real journalist and have a proper career, then I should get a newspaper job. Newspaper jobs were safe and secure! It seems ridiculous to think about now, because I was young and single, so what the heck – and where are those newspapers now?

No opportunity should seem unreasonable. Take anything that seems exciting! Don't play it safe. Things are less predictable than we like to think.

It's been an object lesson in how unpredictable things are, and how other people's scenarios aren't right for you. I couldn't get a newspaper job and the reason was because I was queer. They couldn't hire someone who looked like me, and who had worked for the gay press. And in fact that was my lucky break. I've built a career that seems sustainable – and seems so much more exciting, so much more my own, than if I'd taken a bureau job.

Masha's Object
A bicycle. I have several, and to call me an avid bicyclist would be an understatement. I cycle a couple of hours a day when I can, and when I travel, I carry a folding bicycle with me. I even have an Instagram devoted to finding the perfect bag for my folding bike. I have a summer bike and a winter bike as well as a folding bike. They give me a sense of freedom and a time when I can be alone and think. And a bicycle is an incredible way to see all the cities I travel to.

DR VANESSA OGDEN

Head teacher,
Mulberry School for Girls

DR VANESSA OGDEN

Vanessa Ogden was born in London. She read theology and religious studies at Manchester University, and then went into banking. In the early 90s she changed career, training as a teacher at the Institute of Education in London. Over the past 20 years, Ogden has improved the standard of education in dozens of London's challenging inner-city schools and she won the Women of the Future Inspirational Educator Award in 2009. Since 2006, Ogden has been head teacher at Mulberry School in Tower Hamlets, London's most deprived borough. She has transformed the school into an over-subscribed beacon of education – twice rated 'outstanding' by Ofsted. In June 2015 the school was chosen by Michelle Obama, First Lady of the United States, as the place to launch her Let Girls Learn initiative in the UK.

I started in banking, which is a good job, but I found that it didn't suit me as a person and, after a year, I knew I needed to do something different. I looked at museum work, at UN work, I visited schools and I volunteered to run a youth club.

I decided to go into education, but, after my first day of teaching in the school where I was placed to do my PGCE [Postgraduate Certificate in Education], I was worried. Next day, I went in to my university and everyone was talking about how brilliant teaching was and how much they were looking forward to taking it all on, and I remember sitting in the student bar and contrasting myself with this barrage of enthusiasm and optimism, and thinking, 'I'm really not sure.'

I was concerned about how well I would manage challenging behaviour, because my way of leadership is reflective of the fact that I've never been extrovert. At that point I'd never been very assertive and I was keen to do things holistically, that is to work in a complex way with people, rather than go out front. But I went on to find that it is the generative side of things that is important in teaching. It's not about being extrovert and assertive; it's about creating knowledge and understanding with young people in a classroom, which is effectively your own domain, and that's what I loved. When I saw students who had struggled with something suddenly get it or suddenly feel successful, I felt huge energy and excitement.

I chose to go straight in at the deep end and teach in London. I so wanted students who

found it difficult to engage with education to learn, to get qualified and become economically empowered and independent. Being a generator of possibility underpins the approach that I've taken to headship at Mulberry. It's important to me to bring down the barriers that exist for young people who experience alienation and exclusion because of their race, gender or financial circumstances – all the schools I've taught in have had significant proportions of students on free school meals.

Being a generator of possibility underpins the approach that I've taken to headship at Mulberry.

My whole drive to give young women the power of choice comes from my mother. She had me at 17 and she was a very brilliant, passionate, intelligent woman, who could have gone to university. She was a postal officer and later became a prominent member of the Communication Workers Union. She fought on behalf of workers who had experienced difficulty in their jobs because they had had accidents or been subjected to racism or sexism. I remember her fighting hard on behalf of a cleaner who had been injured at work.

Her early life as a young mother was dedicated, in some very difficult circumstances, to ensuring that I got the best education and had all the things that could equip me to be self-reliant. She always believed that a young woman should have the maximum opportunity to be financially independent and she really wanted me to go to university. I am inspired by her as a pioneer. She was a modern suffragette. The awful thing is that she died very young, at the age of 52, of ovarian cancer, which was diagnosed late. Sadly, she was not alive when I got my headship or my doctorate, but she did see me become a teacher and she was proud. **When the First Lady** was looking for a place to launch her Let Girls Learn campaign in this country, our school was on the shortlist and we were visited by the US Embassy. With my team, I explained why they should pick Mulberry. We really needed her visit to our community because, at the time, a lot of the stories about Tower Hamlets had been about girls going to Syria, and the pressure on girls in this area was significant. So it was important that somebody of Michelle Obama's standing visibly demonstrated that Mulberry students were important, chosen because of their achievements and who they were.

It's not satisfactory that just 27 per cent of women are represented at board level in certain parts of business and industry, and it's not enough to say that it needs to be 30 per cent. It needs to be 50 per cent.

Although girls are educated equally in this country, that doesn't actually translate into equal opportunities later on. It's not satisfactory that just 27 per cent of women are represented at board level in certain parts of business and industry, and it's not enough to say that it needs to be 30 per cent. It needs to be 50 per cent. In secondary education, just 36 per cent of head teachers are women. I don't think that's acceptable. Since 2007, we've been holding women's conferences to provide an opportunity for girls to have access to female role models in one huge injection. Wonderful women come to speak and, among them, girls are able to see someone whom they might like to be in years

to come. Our aim is to create a partnership of equals. Young men and young women should have equal space, visibility and voice.

Vanessa's Object

A mulberry tree. I strongly identify with the mulberry tree after which the school is named. The mythology about the tree is that it was planted by the Huguenots, the first immigrants to Tower Hamlets, but we have had a tree surgeon estimate its age at only 150 years. Nevertheless, the tree is a symbol for the school and the community, for groups of people coming from places of persecution, or coming with nothing to find a better life and seeing Tower Hamlets as a place where they could settle and find creative energy and resources to grow. Mulberry School has been on this site for 50 years but there was a school here before, which was built in the 1900s for the poor. So there has been a sense of social justice about this school for a long time.

The tree is in the courtyard where girls play, the leaves are heart-shaped and students use them to make cards. Sometimes we have Mulberry debates under the tree. It's a place of significance to everyone and Michelle Obama's visit began in the mulberry tree courtyard where we sang and danced for her and gave her gifts of art.

Everything I do for work is about Mulberry School. I don't have children and, in a way, all Mulberry girls are my daughters. My husband feels that this is critical work and, by being supportive, he contributes, too. And recently, he bought a mulberry tree for our back garden!

DR CORI BARGMANN

Neurobiologist, Rockefeller University, and co-chair, BRAIN Initiative

DR CORI BARGMANN

Neuroscientist Dr Cornelia 'Cori' Bargmann leads the Laboratory of Neural Circuits and Behavior at Rockefeller University, New York, where she is a Torsten N. Wiesel Professor and a Howard Hughes Medical Institute Investigator. She studied biochemistry at the University of Georgia and went on to do a PhD in cancer biology at the Massachusetts Institute of Technology, where she worked with cancer researcher Robert Weinberg. Bargmann's thesis research went on to contribute to the development of the drug Herceptin, which is used in the treatment of breast cancer. As a post-doctoral researcher, she began to use the roundworm as a model system and went on to make discoveries that explain how genes, the environment and experience shape behaviour. In 2013 she was appointed co-chair of the advisory committee for Barack Obama's Brain Research through Advancing Innovative Neurotechnologies (BRAIN) Initiative, which investigates brain disorders, such as Alzheimer's and Parkinson's diseases, depression and traumatic brain injury.

I was a child of the 1960s. When I was eight years old, a man landed on the moon. It was a great period for children to be inspired by science. I wanted to be an astronaut and I think all of my friends wanted to be astronauts, too. I remember looking at the moon to see if I could notice a spaceship. I even remember kind of realising that maybe getting really sick on airplanes, which I did, might be a problem for this ambition! I liked to read. I liked to know everything and, in retrospect, that was great for being a scientist. That said, I also loved music and for a while I thought I wanted to be a pianist, which has nothing to do with being a scientist at all.

I want to understand everything – that's why I am a scientist. Now, instead of outer space, I am interested in inner space.

My father was a professor of statistics and computer science. My mother was a teacher. They both spoke five languages and had been professional translators. My mother was born in 1920 and I realise that she would have been able to play out many more of her intellectual interests now than she did then. She stopped working in paid jobs after I was born. So, during my childhood, she did all the things that women did for free back then – she made recordings for the blind and she did Meals on Wheels. She also took her energy as a teacher and a scholar and focused it with laser-like attention on her children. I am the third of four girls and my parents always communicated to us that we could grow up to do anything. One of my sisters is a doctor, one is an English professor and one works in law.

Competition is a creative force. There is nothing that focuses the mind better than a smart competitor, and that's true in any part of life.

Overwhelming curiosity is the driving force of my character. I want to understand everything – that's why I am a scientist. Now, instead of outer space, I am interested in inner space. I feel that, in our era, the brain is the focus for exciting exploration of the unknown, in the way that the moon was in the 1960s. I am one of the people who helped plan the BRAIN Initiative. On a small scale, in my own lab, I hope we might have something useful to say about mental health, about depression and the way that emotional and motivational states make the brain function in different ways. On a large scale, through the BRAIN Initiative, my role is to help thousands of scientists in different places to do something for brain disorders. They say one person in three – that's one member of your family – will have some sort of serious disorder affecting the brain during his or her life, whether it's Alzheimer's, Parkinson's, depression, schizophrenia or autism, so the medical need is tremendous.

I wouldn't pick out one person as my greatest influence – I would say that every day one person makes me think about something in a new way or try something that I wouldn't otherwise have tried.

People say leading a group of scientists is like herding cats, but it's more like being the leader of a wolf pack. You are working with people who are very intelligent, independent, a bit unconventional. Everyone wants to go in the same direction but there are a lot of strong opinions about what that direction is, so a certain amount of growling and tussling occurs along the way. The goal of all scientists is to learn what has not been known, but it is a human endeavour, so sometimes several people are trying to do the same thing and it ends up being a race. Competition is a creative force. There is nothing that focuses the mind better than a smart competitor, and that's true in any part of life.

I feel most proud that some of my students have gone on to be spectacularly successful scientists. I don't have children so maybe my desire to nourish people and help them grow has been channelled into the graduate students in the lab. Another very satisfying thing is that the work I did as a student contributed one step on the path toward the development of one of the very first rational treatments for cancer – Herceptin. Many people were involved, and I was one of them. I am very happy to think that studying something just because you are curious can actually have an impact in patients.

My worm work continues. In your brain, there are 86 billion nerve cells that are processing information at the speed of electricity. There are also 25,000 genes that have built the brain structures, and chemicals travelling through the brain to help it function. Trying to understand how all the different levels of the brain connect to form a single coherent set of actions is something we can do in the simple brain of the worm but not yet in the complex brain of a human.

I think that the secret of my success in science is that I have very good taste in people. I've worked with really smart people at every stage of my career, starting with those who advised me when I was a student and going on to the people who work with me now. So I wouldn't pick out one person as my greatest influence – I would say that every day one person makes me think about something in a new way or try something that I wouldn't otherwise have tried.

Cori's Object

My seven-foot grand piano. I have an attachment to the piano because it reminds me that, besides science, there are other parts of life. My husband is a neuroscientist, too, and, like me, he started by working on other aspects of biology, including cancer biology. We found each other later in life so that makes us appreciate each other more. We both love music and the opera. It's good when you and the person you live with feel the same way about the opera! Everyone in my family played the piano – my sisters, my mother and my father, who was by far the best of us all. My happiest childhood memories are of lying in bed listening to him play Beethoven far into the night. You can take pleasure from music without being a great performer. Now I hardly play at all, but the piano as an object still matters to me.

HELENA MORRISSEY

*CEO, Newton Investment,
and founder, the 30% Club*

HELENA MORRISSEY

Helena Morrissey graduated in philosophy from Cambridge University and began her career in finance at Schroders in New York. She joined the Newton Investment Management company in 1994 and was appointed CEO in 2001. In June 2014 she was appointed chair of the Investment Association, the UK's industry trade body, the members of which manage £5 trillion between them, and in 2015 she was appointed by the Chancellor to the UK's Financial Services Trade and Investment Board. In 2010, Helena founded the 30% Club, a cross-business initiative aimed at achieving 30 per cent women on UK corporate boards. She has been named one of *Fortune* magazine's World's 50 Greatest Leaders, and she was appointed CBE in the 2012 New Year's Honours list.

My philosophy degree has turned out to be much more useful than people might give it credit for – being philosophical is sometimes quite important in the financial world! I fell into my career. I had done double maths and physics at A-level, but after graduating I didn't know what I wanted to do, and at the time it was fashionable to apply to the City. I didn't really know what I was applying for, in all honesty, which is a bit shocking today when young people research their jobs so carefully. I liked the people I met at my interview with Schroders. There was a mix of men and women, and one particularly likeable woman – and I have since learned that if you like the people you are with, you are more likely to enjoy your work. Schroders offered me a job – they took about 20 graduates each year, and didn't designate exactly what you were going to do. Shortly after, I had a call from HR saying an opportunity had arisen for one graduate to go to New York for two years and would I like to do that. So I got a bit of a break, an opportunity to do something different and a chance to learn – sometimes the hard way, by making mistakes. And that's how I fell into fund management.

Maybe it's partly to do with the way the recruitment process works today, but it seems very hard, hyper-competitive, more formal – you need work experience. Back then, there was more emphasis on finding the right personality. I had an unusual background, but my colleagues did too, having studied subjects such as English and history. I think at that age, you can't always know your forte exactly, and some degree of luck is always involved. I think it's a shame a lot of recruitment processes are a bit narrow. We [at Newton] try to take people from a wide variety of backgrounds, not just those with one particular degree – we want lateral thinkers rather than people who have mastered one subject, and we are not alone in that.

It's slightly ironic, given that people are expecting to work longer and longer, that we agonise so much over the initial job-finding – it takes away some of the spontaneity, the openness, the not knowing quite what the job will be like! I would encourage young people not to worry about not being sure what they want to do, but rather to be open to opportunities. Something will appeal and resonate. Your first job isn't a lifelong commitment. A career might feel fulfilling at one point, but things can change. If we are going to be working for 40, maybe even 50 years, that should give us a bit more confidence to take risks, to accept that we might have several careers. I would like to see things a bit more fluid.

I believe strongly that you can create your own opportunities and one way of doing that is by asking for help when you don't have the answers. There are different ways of achieving and learning, and playing to your strengths, but asking for advice and making sure you don't feel completely on your own is important. It's difficult to generalise, but women do tend to take the whole burden on themselves. For men, how they ask for help might be discreet, but they generally have a network they can call on if they're missing something. I've never had a formal mentor, but I believe strongly in the power of mentoring. I have lots of people whose opinions I'm comfortable seeking, who will correct me if I'm wrong – again, openness is important.

I would encourage young people not to worry about not being sure what they want to do, but rather to be open to opportunities. Something will appeal and resonate. Your first job isn't a lifelong commitment.

I totally subscribe to the idea of meritocracy – but the definition of merit can be very narrow. Men develop networks and allegiances; women have a different approach. The 30% Club was born out of frustration that so many women are so capable and that isn't recognised. The homogeneity of boards and management teams was definitely a contributory factor to the financial crisis. People were too insular, they weren't questioning each other, they had been to the same schools, they were friends. This isn't just about women. Men are involved in the 30% Club, too, men on boards who want to see a different boardroom dynamic. We want to further a cultural shift in businesses and organisations.

Our Schoolroom to Boardroom campaign came about because we can't wait until people are one level below the boardroom and hope they haven't left! It's about creating a continuum. It's important to speak in schools – boys' schools as well as girls' schools. I have sons as well as daughters [she has nine children] and it's important to make young people conscious that this issue hasn't been solved yet. I had a few knocks in my earlier career related to my gender, including doubt over my commitment when I had just come back after having a baby. I was shocked! It never occurred to me that my gender would be a factor.

Things are changing. The 30% Club carried out a survey of students' aspirations. No one said they just wanted to make loads of money and 99 per cent, male and female, said a good work/life balance would be a career priority. That term hadn't even been invented when I was a student. Established business has been slow to pick up on this, but young people today expect more. Right from the beginning they want to have a career, have a family, make a difference, make their intellectual contribution any time, any place. I've noticed this not only with my own children but also with their peers. Young men and women both want work/life balance. It's not just a woman's thing. It's how we move on as a society.

Helena's Object
I've chosen my home. Not for the structure itself but for what it holds within – my family. Material objects aren't meaningful to me – it's all about the people I love. My favourite place in the world is home, with those people. When I'm away from home, I always carry a photo of all the family – including, of course, my husband. Currently it's a lovely one from a summer holiday in Portugal on a blustery day; a bit of the essence of everyone's character is in the picture and I smile every time I look at it. The children have given me a beautiful big collage of photos of them each holding up their own version of an 'I love you' message – I'd like a portable version of that to carry with me too.

217

CAROL BECKWITH
& ANGELA FISHER

Photographers of African rituals and ceremonies

CAROL BECKWITH AND ANGELA FISHER

Carol Beckwith, American, and Angela Fisher, Australian, met in Kenya in 1979 and have been working together ever since, photographing African rituals and ceremonies. In the course of creating their extraordinary record, comprising more than half a million images, diaries, field journeys, drawings and video recordings, they have travelled over 300,000 miles, on camels, mules and on foot, in 4x4s and in canoes, visiting 48 countries, living with 150 different ethnic groups and exploring their cultures for weeks or months at a time. They have written 16 books and their photographs have been widely published in magazines and exhibited in museums all over the world.

We met after Carol had taken a hot-air balloon across the Masai Mara. The trip was a birthday present from her family so she could photograph the area from the air, and the balloon's pilot was my brother. At 1,000 feet, he looked deep into Carol's eyes and said, 'There's something I'd like to tell you ...' There was a thrilling pause, and then he said, 'I'd really like you to meet my sister.'

We met in Nairobi months later, and neither of us was what the other one had expected. One of us was in high heels and the other one was wearing a beaded backless dress. There was an immediate bond. [Carol had trained as a fine artist and had been a painter before becoming a photographer. Angela's background was in sociology and she was writing a book about African jewellery.] Within weeks of meeting, we'd had the idea of compiling a visual record of the ceremonies that accompany people through life in Africa.

You almost spring to press the shutter at the decisive moment, to capture the essence of what you're experiencing.

It's very rare to have a 40-year collaboration between women. We spend five to ten months a year in Africa, depending on the stage of our current project. We have to respond to the rhythm of rituals. The Dogon [an ethnic group living in Mali] hold a mask ceremony every ten years to drive the spirits of the ancestors to the afterlife, and the Masai have a ceremony to pass from warriorhood to elderhood once every 14 years. If you want to experience those, you have to be there at the right time, but in Africa everything is on a sliding scale. You can arrive and there won't be enough honeybeer brewed, so you have to wait two months.

The people we work with understand that we come with an appreciation for their cultures and traditions and a deep respect for the creativity in their cultures.

We see things similarly – 99 per cent of the time, we're agreed about what makes the best photograph. We both take the pictures and we share joint credits. We are always trying to raise the standard, so we celebrate each other's photography – but if you looked at a breakdown of our images, you would find that they are split more or less equally between the two of us. It's hard to define what makes a great image but you can sometimes feel it coming; you almost spring to press the shutter at the decisive moment, to capture the essence of what you're experiencing. We are see-ers rather than thinkers. We focus on the moment.

Sometimes we will spend as much as seven months living with a group of people. We don't even take out our cameras for the first few days. We learn some of the language, we make friends and we become part of a family – and then people are happy for you to record them. Increasingly, these days, we get requests, especially from groups who are concerned that their traditions may be dying out. We recently climbed a mountain with the Samburu [an ethnic group living in Northern Kenya], who have never allowed women to come to their ceremonies before, to witness a ritual that has given meaning to generations of men but which the elders now fear may never happen again.

We have always wanted to remind people that there are 1,300 different cultural groups in Africa, reaching some of the great peaks in humankind's creativity.

It is important for us when we take photographs that people don't feel we are taking something away. Reciprocity is an important concept in Africa and we always bring presents, whatever is appropriate – sugar and tea to the desert, fish hooks to the Omo River in Ethiopia – and we always bring back our finished books. We ask the elders what would help them and we have a fund so that we can give them a well or a small clinic, something practical that maintains their independence. Fundraising takes up at least part of every year, because you don't make any money from books. The people we work with understand that we come with an appreciation for their cultures and traditions and a deep respect for the creativity in their cultures.

We feel very strongly that everyone in the world should benefit from progress, and medicine and schooling undoubtedly improve people's lives. But we are also aware that traditional cultures nurture many things that are missing in our world. The individual is not on his or her own. The elders are always included in the community and their wisdom and knowledge is passed down. The ceremonies that are attached to the progression of life are a great preparation for the next stage. We have a friend who attended the Dipo ceremony of the Krobo people [an ethnic group in Ghana], in which girls are taught cooking and dancing and how to present themselves and even ways of making love. She also went to Oxford and she said, of the two, the ritual was of more benefit in helping her to move forward into adulthood.

As well as having a good working relationship, we are friends. It's always been important to both of us to have men in our lives. But we're continually on the move and when you're in a traditional community, you have to be part of that world. We're lucky that we have both found relationships with understanding men but you have to find someone who likes spending time on their own!

When we took our last book back to the Wodaabe [nomadic cattle herders in the Sahel], the chief, who is a very special friend of ours – we have made 20 or 30 visits – spent several hours looking at it. He has seen two or three books in his entire lifetime. Eventually, he said that it was 'medicine not to forget'. We hope that's right, because we have always wanted to remind people that there are 1,300 different cultural groups in Africa, reaching some of the great peaks in humankind's creativity.

Carol and Angela's Object
A Leica camera. That's the one object that sums up our history and our careers. We both started with Leicas and they are very versatile and lightweight. If you need to be mobile, you want something you can carry on your shoulder, even if you've got two of them. You need to have your camera with you all the time because then you can catch the decisive moment when someone is at the peak of emotion. The camera is what enables your eye, your hand and your inner vision to work together and to reach into what it is to be another person, to capture their spirit. It is an amazing thing, to hold the images of your life as you travel through it.

LAURA BATES

Founder of Everyday Sexism Project, writer and activist

LAURA BATES

Laura Bates studied English at Cambridge University and worked as an actor before launching the Everyday Sexism Project in 2012. The project allows women to post online about the sexism they experience in everyday life. It rapidly gathered momentum, reaching 100,000 entries in April 2015, and, as of late 2015, had nearly a quarter of a million Twitter followers and is now active in more than 20 countries across the world. Laura Bates's first book *Everyday Sexism* was published in 2014, and her second book, *Girl Up*, in 2016.

The Everyday Sexism Project started out of a sense of sheer frustration. I had never been involved in the women's movement and wasn't particularly aware of feminism. Then, in just one week in 2012, various things happened: I was followed by a man who was really aggressively propositioning me; some blokes in a car competed over who could shout the worst thing at me; I was groped; a man said 'Look at the tits on that.' I thought about all those incidents and what struck me most forcefully was that I wouldn't have thought any further about any of them in isolation. What brought them home was that they all happened at once. It was the normalisation of casual sexism that struck me – and I wondered why this was such an accepted part of life in 2012.

That prompted me to start asking other women and girls about their experiences. I thought maybe five or six would have a story to tell, but it was everyone – hundreds of stories. But until they were asked, the women I spoke to never told anyone. I started trying to talk about it and people said that sexism didn't exist any more, I needed to learn how to take a compliment, I should look at women elsewhere and realise I didn't have anything to complain about. I just wanted to close that gap between what was happening and what people thought, which was that the problem didn't exist. I thought if all the stories were in one place, other people would have the same epiphany that I'd had, and realise that women weren't complaining about nothing. I thought it would be a tiny website, but it exploded to include people from all over the world, of all ages, genders and sexual identities.

It's amazing to me now that I wasn't aware of feminism. It wasn't that I wasn't interested, or that I rejected it. I just didn't know about it. Social media has enabled so many young women to access feminism and be part of it. The most important thing is the power of collective voices. The reason the project has become important isn't about me. It's about 100,000 voices shouting together. Social media has also made a project that speaks to an audience that isn't self-selecting. A speech, a march, a book – by definition, the people who turn up or read the book are already interested, and are overwhelmingly women. With a quarter of a million people, our posts are being retweeted, reblogged, shared – they are appearing on the pages of people who never went looking for this kind of material. For many men, that's arresting and shocking.

There are, however, two glaring downsides to being on the internet. The first is that not everybody has access to it. We try hard to take the project offline, too – into communities, schools, universities, businesses, government, the police force. The second is online abuse. Those threats have an impact on young women, some of whom are driven out of online spaces. It's not something I've worked out how to cope with. It takes a huge mental toll. The abuse is very graphic and detailed, but I have a lot of support. My husband and family are amazing and I'm trying to deal with it in counselling. And there is a lot of solidarity from other women in the feminist community who've experienced similar things, especially at the beginning, when it came as such an initial shock – like having a bucket of icy water poured over you. Part of you just wants to shut everything down and run away, but you also get pissed off. People are responding to a website on sexual harassment by harassing you in the most sexist way possible: 'There's no such thing as sexism, you stupid bitch!'

What helps most are the success stories, the positives. For every death threat or rape threat, I'll get at least two stories saying a woman has reported a rape, an employer has rethought a policy, girls have set up a feminist society at school. When I started the project, it was hard to feel hopeful about the future, but, because the project has become so well-known and we've created this online community, we're now sharing stories from women who have found ways to stand up. I'm seeing the most incredible energy from young women. It feels as though we're talking about this everywhere now.

I thought maybe five or six would have a story to tell, but it was everyone — hundreds of stories. But until they were asked, the women I spoke to never told anyone.

I'm also hugely aware of, and very grateful for, the work of women who've gone before. Those women have won us enormous gains. We have incredible legislation on equal pay and harassment but the corresponding cultural shift hasn't yet happened. What we need now is the shift in attitudes and behaviours, and that's something legislation can't do. It's up to us as individuals.

I have always been a voracious reader. One of my earliest role models was Malorie Blackman, until recently the UK Children's Laureate. She has a diversity of characters in her books, not just in terms of gender, but also race, which is absent elsewhere. And, more recently, Malala. Her strength of conviction and courage are inspiring to young women all over the world. She showed that you can, at any age, stand up for what you believe in and make a difference.

When you see lists of top women or great women, you often see names you already know. One thing that has become very clear to me is that the real, back-breaking, coalface work in this area is being done by women whose names you never hear. The women who run organisations such as End Violence Against Women, Rape Crisis, Southall Black Sisters — those women are my real inspiration.

Laura's Object
A T-shirt designed by some 12-year-old schoolgirls, who had invited me to speak at their school. The reason was that when they walked into a classroom, the boys had started shouting out numbers in sets of three — seven, five, nine, or eight, four, two and so on. The girls had realised the boys were rating them out of ten for their faces, breasts and bums. I thought the girls who had asked me in might not want to be identified, but when I got there, they were waiting for me, all proudly wearing a T-shirt they had designed, and they had one for me, too. On the front was a quote inspired by Martin Luther King: 'I want to live in a world where I am judged by the content of my character, not the parts of my body.' Often the impact of that kind of behaviour is to shut girls down. I felt so positive that these girls had been able to band together and draw strength from the wider feminist movement. I felt a real surge of hope and admiration. When I took the T-shirt off later, I saw there was also some writing on the back: 'I am 10 out of 10'.

YVETTE VEGA

*Television producer and
co-creator,* Charlie Rose

YVETTE VEGA

Yvette Vega is the executive producer of the popular late-night interview programme *Charlie Rose*, hosted by Charlie Rose and known for its thoughtful mix of topics and its high-calibre, high-profile guests. She has worked on the programme since it was first broadcast in 1991, beginning as Charlie Rose's assistant. She is a graduate of the New York University film school.

People in my team who are in their 20s ask if I knew what I wanted to do when I was their age. I don't think that I did! Sometimes it's good to know what you don't want to do, and that's where I started from. I never pictured myself sitting in an office doing the same duties day to day. I wanted to do something that would make me think creatively. I also knew I didn't want to work alone. I wanted to be part of a team working together. But when I was in my teens, I didn't have anything set in mind. I felt all doors were open and I think that's important. You don't have to choose straightaway.

> *Young people think everything has to be perfect, they have to excel, they can't make a mistake – but if you fall down and scrape your knee, you put on a Band-Aid, get up and run faster!*

My parents were first-generation immigrants – my mother was born in New York, my father in Puerto Rico – and seeing their children gain independence was very important to them. Our mandate at home was to be self-sufficient and find a career where we would not have to struggle financially or take anything from anyone. I loved science and I loved the idea of helping people, so I applied to join New York University's pre-medical programme. It was very rigorous, very competitive, and I just wasn't ready. As a 17-year-old who had always excelled, I felt I was failing. At the time, I saw it as a negative because I didn't make the cut. I did some soul-searching, asked myself what I really loved, took some economics courses, some journalism courses, and when I realised

you could study film-making at the NYU Tisch School of the Arts, I felt like the luckiest person in the world. It was a hard lesson, but it turned out well.

It's OK to make mistakes – that's key. Young people think everything has to be perfect, they have to excel, they can't make a mistake – but if you fall down and scrape your knee, you put on a Band-Aid, get up and run faster! That message doesn't come across often enough. I remember when I was learning to ride my bicycle, I was racing this boy down the block and I hit a crack and fell off. My father was there and rather than saying, 'Let's get an ice cream and go buy something pink,' he said, 'Are you OK? So go get back on the bike and go ride.' That builds your confidence, which is very important for young women. As clichéd as it sounds, experience gives you confidence. You learn over time what works, what's better and what's right.

Mentorship is one of the greatest opportunities for anyone, especially when you are young. When I started working with Charlie Rose, I was 27 and he was 49, two years younger than I am now. The timing was perfect. I was doing a lot of freelance work, maternity-leave cover and temp positions. Charlie was at a crossroads. We met at the right moment. He needed to staff his new programme. I liked fixing things, getting things done, the mechanics of TV. At first I was thinking, 'Someone's assistant? What does that mean? Is this what I went through four years of university for?' But then I met him and we hit the ground running. It was a startup and he shared everything with me. We were really building something, and I got in on the ground floor. There was so much to do, I ended up having all this responsibility from the get-go – 'Call the White House? OK!' I never had a desire for one specific role and doing everything – research, shooting, editing – was perfect. It's a partnership.

I don't know that a work/life balance exists. I look at the high achievers and they've enveloped work into their lives – there's a continuum. There's a very big dilemma here. You get a job offer and you should be able to say, 'Yes, I want to do this, but I also want other things in my life.' People – men and women both – don't really talk about this, and until we have that discussion, we're fooling ourselves if we think there is a work/life balance. It's the responsibility of those who are hiring to say, 'Put that work aside now.' Until that happens, it's not going to change. You can be productive all you want, but if you're not happy in your whole life, the economy and society will suffer. I used to do all-nighters, we never took any vacation, I sometimes thought I was drowning. Had I already been a parent, it wouldn't have worked out – but someone had to do that work. Younger people these days are more willing to say, 'I don't have to take that fast track right now,' and that's healthy. Equally, the person who doesn't have a family shouldn't end up doing all the work.

Some people team–build so that, as a whole, we learn from each other along the path.

I consider myself a collaborator, and I think that is a type of leader. Some people's nature drives them to the front and centre, but that doesn't always denote leading. Some people team-build so that, as a whole, we learn from each other along the path. That is the kind of leader I believe myself to be. Good leaders listen, and good leaders adapt. As situations change, you need to be able to adjust, listen to someone else's way or solution, and that helps you grow as a leader. We all lead in our own lives, or at least that is the goal.

I would say the following to my teenaged self. 'Take chances and listen to yourself. Laugh a lot, smile a lot, talk to strangers and experience the new as much as you can. Do not be afraid about what others think. Don't ever sell yourself short. Believe in yourself and have confidence to make the right choices. It's also important to listen to those around you whom you trust. It's OK to make mistakes. Even if they are big ones, they're just lessons, so learn from them. You never want to go back down the road that has too many thorns or the road that is so dark you cannot see in front of you. Take a buddy along on your adventures – a friend, a romantic interest, a relative – so that you can have shared experiences. Ask opinions of those you admire. They will tell you something you might already sense in yourself but have yet to discover.

Give yourself a break once in a while. Allow yourself to embrace imperfection. Know that you are beautiful inside and out. That knowledge doesn't need to come from anyone other than yourself.

Yvette's Object
A Yashica Electro 35mm film camera. I picked it up when I was about 17 and I loved this camera. It was so simple to use. It became part of me, an extension of what I wanted to say when I could not find the words. I took pictures of things and people I cared for – family, close friends, my pets, landscapes, nature, buildings, city life. I've treasured many objects throughout my life, but the camera defines my passion. The camera is an eye. It's a viewfinder into life. It can also be a safety shield when you do not feel confident. It's a tool that helps guide you. It's also a companion. You are never alone or lonely with a camera.

JUDE KELLY

Artistic director,
Southbank Centre

JUDE KELLY

As artistic director of Britain's largest cultural institution – Southbank Centre – since 2006, Jude Kelly is a significant figure in the arts. She grew up in Liverpool, one of four daughters, and studied drama at Birmingham University. At 22 she founded Solent People's Theatre and Battersea Arts Centre, and in 1990 she became founding director of the West Yorkshire Playhouse, where she spent 12 years. In 1997 she was awarded an OBE, and in 2015 she was made a CBE for services to the Arts. She created the annual WOW – Women of the World – festival, which takes place at the Southbank, in other parts of the UK and in countries all over the world.

When I look in the mirror, I am searching to see if I am content and excited, because whatever you think you are, your eyes will tell you the truth. I'm not looking for obvious things of the 'do I look tired?' variety, but more 'am I being the me that I want to be?' If I see something different from what I've been telling myself, I think about it.

> *I wanted to be creative but other than through occasional school plays, I didn't have a way to control and shape ideas.*

People do tend to paste on to me assumptions about confidence, assertion and determination, because I am a woman working at a senior level. Most of us develop a convenient personality that reassures others we are capable and everything's fine. As I've got older, I've realised that friendship and intimacy, and not just with those closest to us, is helped if you reveal more of your inner landscape, so there is less difference between what's going on inside and what you're showing the world. Vulnerability is a good thing.

My ambitions when I was young are the same as they are now. When I was six, I started making up shows and persuading the neighbourhood children to take part. And that's what I've been doing ever since.

I knew that I wanted to direct from the age of 14, but I didn't come from a background where anybody knew how to get into the arts. I wanted to be creative but other than through occasional school plays, I didn't have a way to control and shape ideas.

The turning point came when my inspirational headmaster, Bill Pobjoy, gave me permission to take over the school hall at lunchtime. I formed a theatre company and, by the time I went to university at 18 to study drama, I was already thinking how I was going to operate professionally. It made me realise that if young people say they want to do something, they probably mean it, and helping them to get on with it is really important.

My father made me feel that I should do whatever I believed I could do. A civil servant, he was committed to the idea of training and education for himself and his daughters. Later on, architect Cedric Price influenced my sense of courage. He was interested in using buildings to maximise their potential in society and my work has been not just creating art and giving rein to cultural ideas, but forming a sense of place that's relevant. When I take over buildings, such as the Southbank Centre, I challenge the space to speak about what's happening now.

> *It's hubris to imagine that you can organise your life as if you are in charge, because fate will play a part.*

When you are a leader, being a good storyteller is helpful, because you can describe future ideas in a way that will excite people. You have to imagine the place you're aiming for and work backwards in order to chart the path. You can't just fling an idea forward.

But doing all the talking isn't leadership – you have to listen, share your vision and be pleased when people do different as well as complementary things. I am good at spotting those who have potential and then giving them space to get going. You don't want people cloned in your image or who tell you that everything you are doing is right. Leadership needs to be stimulated through challenge.

The project I am most proud of is a play that I did with Nigerian writer Wole Soyinka. He had to flee from the Abacha regime and asked if I would go to Nigeria while he was in exile, work with actors and bring them to the UK to put on a play that he'd written. It was a demanding assignment, bordering on the dangerous, but I put on *The Beatification of Area Boy* at the West Yorkshire Playhouse in 1995, and it was one of those rare moments when art provides a platform for conversations around the world.

In this country, there is more acknowledgement now that women direct, design and produce. On the other hand, there is less money and less obvious opportunity. Oxbridge and the public-school route still count inordinately, because of the massive distortion in our education system with regard to boys and girls from different backgrounds.

There is also still an issue of confidence among women. You inherit confidence over generations of leadership role models and women haven't had that, so there is further to go. I mentor women to have the confidence to become leaders of organisations or to remain in leadership. Women can lose courage, partly because of practical pressure, if they are juggling with childcare problems for instance.

> *You inherit confidence over generations of leadership role models and women haven't had that, so there is further to go.*

I have two children who are now 27 and 25, and are, respectively, a poet and a choreographer. Being a parent adjusts your priorities and your sense of self, and that is a wonderful thing. It's hubris to imagine that you can organise your life as if you are in charge, because fate will play a part. The loss of my son Johnny when he was three months old was terrible, but it made me much more accepting of not being able to control everything and more loving of the things I had.

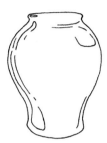

Jude's Object

A simple white porcelain pot, which I purchased on a trip to Japan eight years ago. A close friend took me to see a potter who had spent his whole life throwing fine white porcelain, which is a difficult thing to do. Each pot is an extraordinarily pure luminous white and totally individual, and I bought one. It's ornamental, the size of a medium vase, but so beautiful, it doesn't need a flower.

The potter isn't throwing pots to be world famous. His endeavour is philosophical. We talked about the challenge of throwing over and over again, knowing you would never get a perfect pot because there is no such thing, and if there was, it wouldn't necessarily be interesting. He had experimented with colour and different glazes but kept taking them off, thinking, 'This in itself is enough.'

My pot is so simple but the result of years of work, and it encapsulates many of the things that I believe in. In my work, I attempt over and over again to give individual recognition to a person or a moment, and each has its own meaning and beauty just because of what it is. In life we have to hold on to things lightly. It's just possible that, somewhere along the line, I might lose my white porcelain pot, but whether or not I have it physically, what it represents will always be with me.

MAJORA CARTER

Urban revitalisation strategist

MAJORA CARTER

Majora Carter is an urban revitalisation strategy consultant, real-estate developer and Peabody Award-winning broadcaster. She gained a film studies degree at Wesleyan University and a Master of Fine Arts at New York University. After returning to her native South Bronx, she worked for the Point Community Development Corporation and ran a successful campaign to stop 40 per cent of New York's municipal waste being deposited at a planned facility in the area. She also transformed a rubbish dump into Hunts Point Riverside Park. In 2001 she founded the non-profit organisation Sustainable South Bronx (SSBx) to champion green job training, community greening programmes and social enterprise. Since leaving SSBx in 2008, Carter has formed the economic consulting and planning firm Majora Carter Group to bring her pioneering approach to other communities.

I am the youngest of ten and all my siblings had huge presence. They were athletes and performers, and they were popular. I wasn't. I was funny looking and I liked to read and be alone. I looked at them and thought, 'Oh, that's what you're supposed to be,' not this weird kid who likes to play with rocks and dig up bugs in the backyard. So, as a teenager, I wanted to be popular, I wanted to be an extrovert and I wanted to be an actress because I wanted to be seen. But when I was in college, I realised I was an introvert and I didn't want any of that any more.

As a teenager, I wanted to be popular, I wanted to be an extrovert and I wanted to be an actress because I wanted to be seen. But when I was in college, I realised I was an introvert and I didn't want any of that any more.

My mother was a homemaker. My father was 21 years older than my mom and, by the time I was five, he was retiring from his job as janitor at the juvenile detention facility around the corner from our house. That place is now vacant – no children there any more, thank God – and I'm on a team competing to redevelop it into a mixed-income housing and mixed-use commercial site. I think my father would be proud that his daughter is trying to dismantle something that he knew was a terrible place.

The site is one of the largest redevelopments in New York City and the language that the city has used to guide developers in terms of their work is all about 'transformation' and 'social cohesion' and 'environmental equality'. That was language that I used and they incorporated in order to make sure that whatever development happened would happen in a wonderful way. Of course I want my team to win, but if we don't, I know that I've set the standard for what excellence can be in a low-income community of colour, and that makes me delighted.

When you're a leader, you have to know when to get out in front and when to fall behind. I go out in front when I know a project is going to work, even though it might seem crazy or I am not getting support. An example is StartUp Box, a social enterprise that involves people in low-status communities in the tech economy. One of the things we do is develop software services for the tech industry. This project has been incubated under an NGO [non-governmental organisation], so there is a philanthropic part, but otherwise it is straight business development and that is what folks in the investment world had absolutely no faith in. None whatsoever! And I said, 'We've done the market research, we know this is a great idea and we've got to do it.' And we did.

As a leader, the time to fall behind is when you are trying to raise others up and give them the courage to make mistakes so that they can step up their game. It's what the late activist Yolanda Garcia did for me, and I still consider her a guiding light. I was working at the Point, she for the organisation that she founded, but we were working for the community together. I considered myself Tonto to her Lone Ranger. I would research for her; I would go over briefs with her; she would say something and I would back it up. She was the leader and I was fine with that, I didn't want to be out in front. But she pushed me and said, 'This is your community, too. Speak for it.'

People don't know that I am often not comfortable in the place that I'm in. I do it because I have no choice – I can't be a shrinking violet and do this work. I've got to step out and I know that my example inspires people, particularly women. My teenaged self would have loved that – maybe she was more in touch with me than I gave her credit for!

My husband, James [Chase], has been the kind of supporter whom I didn't know existed. He is president of StartUp Box, vice president of communications in my consulting firm and my best friend. He lifts me up when I can't move any more. He describes his role as that of coach to a boxer who is getting beaten up. He gives me a pep talk and makes me go right back out into the ring.

When you're a leader, you have to know when to get out in front and when to fall behind. I go out in front when I know a project is going to work, even though it might seem crazy or I am not getting support.

We married in Hunts Point Riverside Park on 7 October 2006. The first time I saw the place was in 1998, when my dog pulled me into a horrible dump by the river. By 2000 there was no garbage and no more dumping and we had some trees and nice rock formations, and by 2004 we'd got the full amount – $3 million – to transform the park totally. In 2006 it was done and we got married there on the first day it was open. It was beautiful.

I am almost 50 years old and I am working harder than at any other point in my life. I want to be able to take a break and enjoy all these beautiful things that I've built. But the idea of using real-estate development as a transformational tool for social, environmental and economic equality is not normal, so I have to continue until it is. Then I can take a break.

Majora's Object

Oscar the Grouch from *Sesame Street*. The great American television series dominated my childhood. I loved it more than anything and my favourite character was Oscar the Grouch, who lived in a trash can. He didn't like people but there was something about him and I loved him more than any of the characters that were warm and fuzzy. I was drawn to this curmudgeon of a person, who actually wasn't a bad guy. He was honest and good and he taught me that you can't judge a book by its cover.

Recently, StartUp Box made a client out of Sesame Workshop, the folks who run the show. They have a gift shop and James bought me an Oscar the Grouch plush toy and I love it. James has tried to analyse me about my love of Oscar and I think there is something in it. Oscar has beauty underneath. I feel that you just have to uncover beauty, or help it along, but it is always there and, when you find it, it helps you to see yourself in that way. For me that is a big deal.

VANESSA FRIEDMAN

Fashion director,
New York Times

VANESSA FRIEDMAN

Vanessa Friedman was born in New York and studied at Princeton University. She became a journalist and wrote for magazines, such as *Vanity Fair* and US *Elle*. In 1996, she and her husband moved to the UK and she went on to work for the *Economist* and *InStyle*. She also freelanced for the *Financial Times* before becoming their first fashion editor in 2003. In 2014 she left the FT and took up her current post as fashion director and chief fashion critic of the *New York Times*. She is known for her incisive socio-political commentary on the role of fashion in our lives. In 2010, she published her first book, a celebration of the life and work of Italian designer Emilio Pucci.

When I was growing up, I wanted to be a lawyer, then a neurosurgeon. I thought about being a chemist for a while, and an astronaut. At Princeton I studied history and wasn't interested in fashion. I thought it frivolous and superficial in the way that intellectually pretentious 20 year olds do. When I graduated, I worked for a law firm in Paris for a year and a half because I was thinking about going to law school, but I was also considering journalism. In the end, I decided that I could still go to law school if I didn't like magazines, but I was never going to get into magazines as a 40-year-old editorial assistant!

My mother was a book editor and then a literary agent. She was very much a mother but also a professional, and successful at a time when there were not a lot of women in her profession.

I worked at a variety of magazines and culture was always my focus – I liked books and film and TV. Then, in London, I started freelancing for the *Financial Times* and that's where I first wrote about fashion. When they decided to have a fashion editor in 2003, it coincided with me going back to work after the birth of my second child, and I got the job.

Part of what was fantastic about the job at the FT was being able to define fashion in a way that glossy magazines and other newspapers didn't already do. And I feel similarly about the *New York Times*. The people who read these newspapers care about fashion but clothes are not the guiding principle of their lives. Their lives are about lots of other things and so our job is to show them where the choices they make about clothes intersect with the choices they make about a whole host of other areas with which they may be more familiar.

I feel strongly about professional women being up-front about the different roles they play in their lives.

My parents were my formative influence. They gave me my value systems and guided me. When I was growing up, my father was a corporate lawyer who went into government, and my mother was a book editor and then a literary agent. She was very much a mother but also a professional, and successful at a time when there were not a lot of women in her profession. She dealt with all the prejudices and gender stereotypes that we hear about and that, to a certain extent, still exist, although not in the same form. I remember her telling me that she was in a salary negotiation and somebody said to her, 'Why do you need more money? You have a successful husband.' **My mother gave me** a very important piece of advice – you can have it all, just not necessarily at the same time. And I think, as a woman

The important thing in life is to be curious and open to possibilities.

trying to balance family and work and travel and hobbies, that is absolutely correct. You make choices depending on what's going on in your life at different times. I never doubted that I came first, despite both my parents having full-time jobs, and that is what I want for my children – I have two daughters and a son. I feel strongly about professional women being up-front about the different roles they play in their lives. So I will say to employers, 'I have to go to my kid's graduation,' or, 'I can't come in today, my son is sick.' Getting these issues out there is important, not just for women but also for men. It is our responsibility to acknowledge the challenges that everyone faces in family life and work life so that they are part of the conversation, and to demonstrate that you can be professional and have everything in on time – and go to the school play.

I will say to employers, 'I have to go to my kid's graduation,' or, 'I can't come in today, my son is sick.'

The advice I would give my teenaged self is the same advice that I give my kids – when you are growing up, some of it sucks and some of it's brilliant, and that's actually what's interesting about it all. When I was going through school, there was still a sense of career paths – you studied x and it led to y – but that is not the case any more. One of the things I said recently to the graduating class at Parsons [School of Design in New York] is that we've created a very messy, very scary world. Competition comes from all sorts of unexpected places but, also, opportunities that you couldn't even imagine, and that's incredibly exciting. The important thing in life is to be curious and open to possibilities. If you had told me when I was 18 or 21 that I would be a fashion critic on

a newspaper, I would have told you, in not very polite terms, that you were very wrong, and that shows just how wrong I was.

Vanessa's Object
A trapeze bar. My hobby is the flying trapeze and, like my career in fashion, it's something that I came to relatively late and I love it. The flying trapeze requires a lot of the same qualities as a career – the willingness to jump in unexpected directions, the need to listen to and trust other people (you have to trust your catcher) and exposure to a different world that's fascinating and populated by all sorts of characters.
I started the trapeze when I moved back to the US from the UK. My middle daughter was in kindergarten and another mother said that it would be a good thing for the kids to do, to get over their fear of heights. So she arranged a class and I took both my daughters. All the kindergarten kids were horrified, but I thought it looked fun and, with my elder daughter, I carried on and I am in better shape than I have been in my entire life.
The flying trapeze is not the easiest hobby to work into your daily schedule and it's like being part of a secret society of circus people. Shoe designer Christian Louboutin has a little trapeze studio in Paris and we have done a class or two together. In London there is a rig in Regent's Park in summer or I go to the circus school at the Roundhouse in Camden. Last time I was there an instructor told me about a rig in Milan so, when I was at fashion week there, I played hooky – and it really cleared my head!

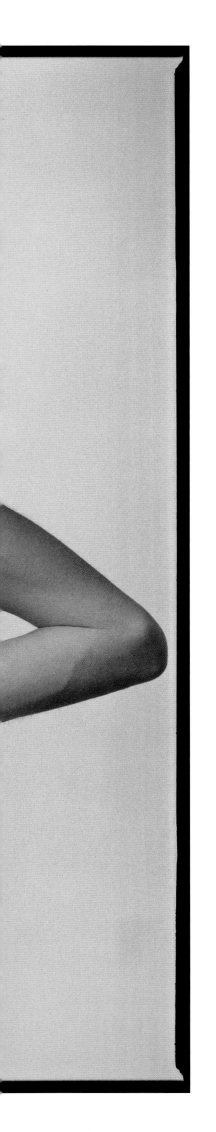

ASHIMA SHIRAISHI

Rock climber

ASHIMA SHIRAISHI

Ashima Shiraishi is a world champion rock climber. She was born in New York in 2001, the daughter of Japanese immigrants, and won her first competition at the age of seven. She went on to win the American Bouldering Series Youth National Championship for five consecutive years, excelling at climbing without ropes and harnesses. In 2015 she set records when she climbed the Open Your Mind Direct route at Santa Linya in Spain, becoming the first female and the youngest person to have achieved a climb of this difficulty. In the 2015 Golden Pitons she was named Climber of the Year. If climbing is accepted as a medal sport, she hopes to compete at the 2020 Olympics in Tokyo.

I started rock climbing when I was six years old in Central Park in New York City. One day I was playing at a playground in the park and I saw people climbing on this big rock. I was really interested and started to do it, too. I kept on falling but every day I went back. I had no climbing shoes so I just wore sneakers.

Once I have done one hard climb I always look for a harder one and keep on pushing my limit because that's what climbers do.

I climb on outdoor rocks and mountains. I also do competitions on artificial rock but I prefer real rock climbing. Climbing is exhilarating. You go up so high and sometimes it's scary, but the fear is an exciting feeling, and when you get to the top, it's the best feeling. I have fallen countless times but that's what makes it so special when you get to the top.
I do two types of climbing. One is free climbing [bouldering], which means that it's only me and the rock. There is nothing to help me – only chalk for my hands but no harnesses or ropes. You climb a rock that's about 15 feet, so not too high. I also do sport climbing where you climb 100 or more feet and you wear a harness and a rope and someone's belaying you [the technique of securing the climber during a climb]. They are both climbing but they are very different. One is like a marathon whereas the other is like a sprint.

Climbing is so natural for me, it's almost like dancing on the rock. Since my dad was a dancer, I feel I naturally have that movement inside me. Sometimes it's almost like flying up the wall and sometimes you actually do fly through the air to grab on to rocks. When I am climbing, I try not to be nervous. A lot of people get really stressed and when you're like that it's hard to climb because there are so many things going on in your mind.

Climbing is exhilarating. You go up so high and sometimes it's scary, but the fear is an exciting feeling, and when you get to the top, it's the best feeling. I have fallen countless times but that's what makes it so special when you get to the top.

Rock climbing is pretty dangerous. You can die and you can definitely get injured so it's a risky sport. But if you pay attention and are aware of what you are doing and are focused, then you're fine. I haven't got injured but I have a lot of callouses on my fingers and my feet from rock climbing. Sometimes I get scared when I am high up in the air, but most of the time I am relaxed and composed. Of course, when you are falling, it's definitely not fun – you are frustrated. But during those times I just think about getting to the top and how I will feel when I get there.

Once I have done one hard climb I always look for a harder one and keep on pushing my limit because that's what climbers do. Climbing is both a physical and a mental sport. You really have to think when you're climbing, so you have to be smart. First you have to see the path that you're going to take – that's one of the most important parts. You look at the climb and see where you are going to put your hands and then you look at where you're going to put your feet and how your body is going to be positioned. You can never 100 per cent know what you are going to do, though. I always improvise along the way, because you can't look at a climb from the bottom and have it perfectly, so as you are climbing you change your sequence. People have told me that I have a high climbing IQ so I can see the sequence very easily and I do sequences that no one else imagines.

Physical strength is important but the most important thing is good concentration. I feel like climbing has made me a more disciplined person and, even at school, it shows.

I love to do competitions and I love to travel round the world. It's definitely hard to manage school and climbing. I wake up at 6.30 in the morning and I go to school until 3.30. I go to climbing gym from four till eight, then I go back home, eat dinner and do homework. When I go to sleep it's about 1am so it's a hard schedule. I care about school and I love to learn but homework is definitely one of my challenges! My dream is to keep on climbing and I want to push the female boundaries of rock climbing and maybe have females dominating the sport. Physical strength is important but the most important thing is good concentration. I feel like climbing has made me a more disciplined person and, even at school, it shows. Sometimes I want to stop climbing because there is so much going on in my life and I just

want to be like anyone else, but I always return to it because I just love it so much. If I don't do it, then it feels like I am losing something. I have two worlds – friends at school who don't climb and friends from the climbing world. I like to hang out with my friends from school and just be a normal teenager, going to movies and figure skating.

Both my parents are very supportive and I am the only child. My father coaches me and, because he used to be a dancer, he has helped me to move more delicately on the rock and really understand how to keep my core tight and how to prepare mentally. My mom makes all my climbing pants and sometimes she comes to competitions with me, too. I hope to be in the 2020 Olympics in Tokyo. As a little girl my dream was to be in the Olympics.

Ashima's Object
My unique climbing pants. They are what I treasure most in life, the comfortable, loose pants that I always climb in. My mom hand-makes my pants and my father chooses the fabric, which either comes from Japan or is Japanese-inspired. Since no one else in the world has the same pair of pants, I believe that I stand out and, as I have been wearing them since I began climbing, they are a part of me. And when I'm not with my parents, I receive their power from the pants!

ABOUT THE PROJECT

The Female Lead is a not for profit project.

Many of the books, and all of the films and teaching materials are being donated to schools and universities via trusted networks in the UK and USA.

On books sold, all royalties will go back into the project to fund further materials to be donated to schools.

We would like to hear from any organisation that can help us bring this to more countries and more young people around the world.

www.thefemalelead.com

@female_lead

SALLIE KRAWCHECK

SUCCESS AND FAILURE
ARE VIEWED
AS END POINTS,
NOT A PROCESS.
IN FACT, YOU MIGHT
BE A FAILURE
ONE DAY, BUT YOU CAN
STILL BE A SUCCESS
THE NEXT. YOU CAN FAIL
AND SUCCEED
EVERY DAY.

THE EXPECTATIONS
PLACED ON
YOUNG WOMEN
BY BOTH SOCIAL MEDIA
AND TRADITIONAL MEDIA
ARE IMPOSSIBLE TO
NAVIGATE, BUT I SEE A
NEW GENERATION
FIGHTING BACK
AND IT GIVES ME A LOT
OF HOPE.

LENA DUNHAM

DR MAGGIE ADERIN-POCOCK

TAKE YOUR
DREAMS
TO THE STARS,
BE AN
OPPORTUNIST,
SEE HOW FAR
YOU
CAN GET.

RARELY DOES A DAY
GO BY WHEN
I DON'T DISCOVER
A WOMAN
WHO INSPIRES ME,
RIGHT ACROSS
THE GENERATIONS,
FROM 16 YEAR OLDS TO
OCTOGENARIANS.

PROF NAZNEEN RAHMAN

ACKNOWLEDGEMENTS

I would like to thank the following people for inspiration, connectivity and masses of practical help:

For bringing the book and films to life
Brigitte Lacombe, Photographer,
Marian Lacombe, Film-maker
Bea Appleby, Editor
Prof. Phil Cleaver, Designer
Hester Lacey, Journalist
Geraldine Bedell, Journalist
Rosanna Greenstreet, Journalist
Dr Terri Apter, Psychologist and Writer
Amber Cooper-Davies, Illustrator
Janet Johnson, President, Lacombe Inc.
Isabelle Steinl, Video Editor
Emily Lord, Aidan Jones, Jennifer Penny,
et al design consultants
Carey Smith, Publishing Director, Ebury
Lydia Good, Editor, Ebury

The written profiles of Ava DuVernay, Samantha Power, Meryl Streep, Laurene Powell Jobs, Karlie Kloss, Christine Lagarde, Ashima Sharaishi, Vian and Deelan Dakhil Saeed were taken from Marian Lacombe's video interviews

The Female Lead team
Martha Rampley, Laura Whiteside,
Veryan Dexter, Eve Simmons and
Samantha Fosbury

The Lacombe team
Vanessa Gomez, Studio Manager
Hanna Bradbury, Assistant Studio Manager
Lanny Jordan Jackson, Archivist

Molly Welch, Exhibitions Manager
TJ Huff, Post-production & Printer
David Coventry, Photo Assistant
Shane Nelson, Photo Assistant

For helping us to develop our campaign
Jane Quinn at Bolton & Quinn, Nick Keegan,
Michael Hayman and Nick Giles at Seven Hills,
Jeff Boardman, Robbie Newby and Rowena
Humby for the What I See project

For helping us to connect
Elizabeth Kesses and Dominique Delport
Tina Brown Live Media, Domino Pateman and
Joanna Newell at Southbank Centre,
Jamila Deria at the Apollo Theatre in Harlem,
Shanaz Begum at Mulberry School in London,
David Vannier and Bruno Silvestre at the IMF,
Hagar Chemali and Kurtis Cooper at the U.S.
Mission to the UN, John Barker and Andrew
Davies at Demeter, David Giampaolo at Pi
Capital, Sylvie Bermann Ambassador of France
to the U.K., Raphaëlle Rodocanachi Cultural
Attachée at Institut Français U.K.

Our Photoshoot Producers
From No Wheelies Patricia Whaley and
Elizabeth Johnson
From NorthSix Maria Domican and Matt Malby

Hair and Makeup stylists
Carolyn Gallyer, Rosie Lewis, Kuma

Every woman in the book was interviewed on film by Marian Lacombe. These videos can all be seen at www.thefemalelead.com